Facts about
NORWAY

25th edition

Norway

Norway is a country full of unspoiled nature, fjords and mountains. Mild winters and relatively high levels of precipitation are favourable for growing conditions, and forests are found almost as far north as Nordkapp (the North Cape).

In spite of economical recession in recent years, Norway is a country of socio-economic equality with a high standard of living and a homogeneous population.

The sea along the coast is rich in natural resources like oil and fish. There are wide open spaces and plenty of fresh air. The total area is about the same size as Great Britain, Germany or Italy. However, the population is a mere 4.5 million, or about half that of London.

Apart from Oslo and adjacent suburbs, there are no metropolitan cities in Norway. Norwegians usually live in small communities with well developed road, air and ferry communication. Many communities are built up around one major business or industrial enterprise.

Contents

Land and People

The Country

Norway (originally Nordweg, "The Northern Way") forms the western part of the Scandinavia and comprises 40 % of the peninsula's total land area. Along 2,531 km, Norway shares borders with Sweden, Finland and Russia. Excluding the fjords, the Norwegian coastline measures an impressive 2,650 km. In addition there are approximately 50,000 islands along the coast.

The capital city of Oslo is situated at latitude of 60° N. Hammerfest, the northernmost town in the world, is located at 70°39'89" N latitude. The Arctic Circle can almost be used to separate Northern and Southern Norway.

Natural Resources

Apart from fish and petroleum, Norway is not particularly rich in natural resources. Oil production is the most important source of income, and petroleum represents approximately 30 % of all Norwegian export. On an international scale, fisheries are also a significant resource.

There is a limited amount of cultivated land in Norway, and in spite of expansive coniferous forest, forestry is also limited. Moreover, Norway is poor in most minerals and metals.

Nevertheless, Norway is one of the richest countries in the world, mainly due to extensive industrialisation, easy access to hydroelectric power, and close proximity to important export markets in Europe.

Topography

Norway is a mountainous country where approximately half of the land area is comprised of the eroded bedrock remains from mountain ranges. The Norwegian landscape varies from pre-Ice Age, horizontal, land formations, to steep perpendicular elements created by glacial activity.

During the last 2–3 million years repeated glaciation effected most of Scandinavia in a manner similar to the continent of Antarctica today. Icy streams flowing toward the coast carved deep crevasses with perpendicular walls in ancient valley floors. Local glaciers, eroding the cirques in old mountainous land masses, transformed them into sharp ridges and peaks.

From the inland mountains and mountain plateaus, the landscape falls sharply toward the coast. Along coastal fjords, alpine mountains resemble drowned giants emerging from the surface of the sea. An undulating lowland along the outer coast is protected from the Norwegian Sea in most places by innumerable islands.

Climate

Due to the country's longitudinal size and geographic conditions, there are vast climatic variations in Norway. The prevailing westerly winds reach fur-

Fjords and steep mountains – many tourists come to Norway in order to experience the typical Norwegian landscape. The picture shows fruit trees in bloom in Gudvangen in the county of Sogn og Fjordane.

ther north in Norway than anywhere else in Europe. The moisture they carry from the sea causes abundant precipitation. The mildness of these winds is due to the North Atlantic Current, better known as the "Gulf Stream".

The coastal climate varies little in average temperature throughout the year. Summers are somewhat cool due to frequent rain and cloudiness, and winters are remarkably mild, with average January temperatures from about 2 degrees Celsius (35.6 °F) in

the Southwest and West, to –6° C (21.2 °F) in the North.

In inland areas, summers are warmer and sunnier, and the winters colder, with snow prevailing for several months. Temperatures may drop well below –30 degrees Celsius (–22 °F) with a record low of –51.4 degrees Celsius (–60.5 °F) measured in inner Finnmark. The mountains in South Norway separate West and East Norway and block most of the moisture from the sea. Therefore, summer in the interior is often quite dry.

On average, the climate of mainland Norway is more clement than would be expected, given latitudes from 58° N near Kristiansand to 71° N at North Cape. The mean annual temperature in Lofoten is a full 25 degrees Celsius (45 °F), higher than normal for this latitude – the highest positive anomaly in the world. Along the coast, broad-leaved deciduous trees thrive as far north as 64° N latitude. Pine, birch and Norwegian spruce can grow as far north as 70° – compared to the western coast of the Atlantic, where forest is not seen further north than 54°. Polar bears strolling in the streets are pure myth. The only polar bears in mainland Norway are the stuffed ones occasionally seen – and photographed – outside hotels and stores.

However, polar bears are common on Svalbard, an arctic island belonging to Norway. Even there, mild ocean currents contribute to a surprisingly mild climate, but the summers are short and cool, and trees do not grow.

Flora and Fauna

Norway's flora is richer than might be expected containing some 2,000 species. Most of these plants are also found in other countries, with the exception of a several mountain plants that are specific to Norway.

The most common trees in

A frosty view of the Oslo harbour on a winter's day.

There is a saying that Norwegians are born with skis on their feet. That is not entirely true, but many Norwegians spend a lot of their spare time out in the nature. Many of the skiing tracks are illuminated, thus they can also be used in the evenings.

Norwegian forests, which cover nearly one-quarter of the country, are spruce and pine. However, there are also many birches and other deciduous trees, even in mountainous districts. The vegetation is richest in the southeastern part of the country, where deep forests in major valleys are the basis of the Norwegian lumber industry. Conifers are seldom found above 800–1,000 metres above sea level.

Likewise, the marine fauna is of considerable importance to the country, in that large districts are more or less dependent on fisheries. There are fresh-water fish, such as trout, in most rivers and lakes in the country, while salmon are rarely caught outside "salmon rivers".

Of land animals, the bear is nearly extinct, while the moose is mainly found in Southeastern Norway and Trøndelag. The reindeer is the most important domestic animal in Finnmark. The largest stock of wild reindeer in Norway is found on Hardangervidda. There are many species of carnivorous mammals, such as the wolf, fox, lynx and otter. Game birds are found in valleys and mountains alike; the ptarmigan (grouse) is the most common of these.

Multitudes of seabirds nest on the coast of Northern Norway. Nesting cliffs on the western and northern coasts, which are inhabited by thousands of sea birds, are a major tourist attraction.

Many migratory birds breed in Norway during the summer, but live in more southerly latitudes the rest of the year. Certain species of fish, such as the mackerel, also migrate. All animals are protected by law and may only be hunted during designated periods or by special permission.

The Midnight Sun

Northern Norway is known to tourists as the "Land of the Midnight Sun". North of the Arctic Circle, the sun shines day and night for part of the summer. In Bodø, just north of the Circle, the midnight sun is visible from June 7–July 8, and there is no daylight from December 15–29th. At North Cape the midnight sun is visible from May 14 to July 29 and the period of darkness lasts from November 18 to January 24.

The darkness is by no means total. The sun is so near the horizon that the "Nordic light" illuminates the landscape. The moon spreads its silver light and the stars sparkle. The Aurora Borealis shines and waves like swords and airy curtains in reds, greens and violets.

Environmental Protection

In accordance with the Environmental Protection Act, any alterations to the environment may only be made in line with principles of the long-term management of environmental resources. Modern environmental protection is not simply a matter of protecting certain areas or cultural artefacts. Consideration of the environment must be integrated into all aspects of government planning.

In 1972, Norway was the first country in the world to establish a Ministry of the Environment. Subsequently, divisions were set up in each county administration. Pollution control is a vital task for the Ministry of the Environment.

Some pollution originates from Norwegian industry, agriculture and domestic settlements. However, the

Summers in Norway can be relatively warm. When the sun comes out, a lot of people enjoy cold refreshments at the many outdoor restaurants.

vast majority of pollution in Norway today is "long range transported" pollution "imported" from other countries through wind and ocean currents. Considerable effort has been made to reduce the damage caused by acid precipitation in Southern Norway. Unlike basic limestone in many other European countries, the acid nature of the predominant bedrock in Norway prevents neutralisation of pollutants.

In some parts of Northern Norway, pollution from Russia has become a serious problem. On several occasions, the Nordic countries have attempted to co-operate with Russian authorities in creating measures for restricting pollution.

In spite of certain environmental problems, Norway's air and water are among the cleanest in Europe.

National Parks

A nation-wide plan for establishing national parks is nearing completion. There are 18 national parks in mainland Norway (1999) and three on Svalbard. Parks on the mainland cover a total area of 13,800 km² (4,25 % of the Norwegian mainland), while Svalbard parks cover a total of 9,500 km².

In principle, Norwegian national parks are large continuous areas of unspoiled, or nearly pristine, wilderness protected against technical encroachment. The objective is to safeguard outdoor life and preserve biological diversity.

National parks encompass landscapes representative of most natural biotopes in Norway, with the exception of coastal areas.

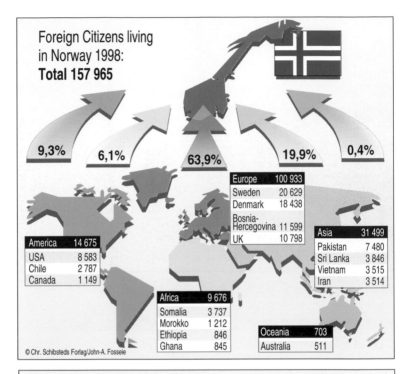

Foreign Citizens living
in Norway 1998:
Total 157 965

9,3%   6,1%   63,9%   19,9%   0,4%

Europe	100 933
Sweden	20 629
Denmark	18 438
Bosnia-Hercegovina	11 599
UK	10 798

America	14 675
USA	8 583
Chile	2 787
Canada	1 149

Asia	31 499
Pakistan	7 480
Sri Lanka	3 846
Vietnam	3 515
Iran	3 514

Africa	9 676
Somalia	3 737
Morokko	1 212
Ethiopia	846
Ghana	845

Oceania	703
Australia	511

© Chr. Schibsteds Forlag/John-A. Fosseie

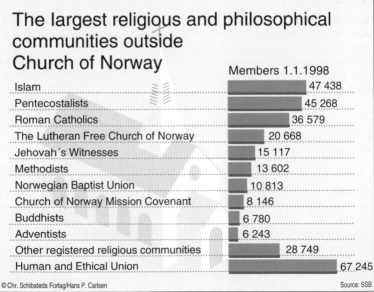

The largest religious and philosophical communities outside Church of Norway

Members 1.1.1998

Islam	47 438
Pentecostalists	45 268
Roman Catholics	36 579
The Lutheran Free Church of Norway	20 668
Jehovah´s Witnesses	15 117
Methodists	13 602
Norwegian Baptist Union	10 813
Church of Norway Mission Covenant	8 146
Buddhists	6 780
Adventists	6 243
Other registered religious communities	28 749
Human and Ethical Union	67 245

© Chr. Schibsteds Forlag/Hans P. Carlsen   Source: SSB

An old Norwegian fishing village. This is from Smøla in the county of Møre og Romsdal.

The People

Population

As of January 1999, the population of Norway approached 4,445,329, or the equivalent of 13.6 inhabitants per square kilometre. If the mainland were divided equally among all inhabitants, there would be some 73,000 m² for each Norwegian. Approximately 75 % of the population live in towns and urban areas (January 1999). The remaining percentage inhabit rural districts.

The majority of the population is of Nordic descent. The Sámi people form an ethnic minority of some 40,000 individuals, mostly in the north. Their culture and language are distinct to that of the rest of Norway.

In today's Norwegian society, various nationalities and ethnic groups are represented.

Religion

The state church has roots dating back to the introduction of Christianity in Norway ca. 1,000 A.D. 88 % of the population belong to the Church of Norway (1995), which is Evangelical-Lutheran. The pietistic movement and missionary activity have long traditions.

Only 3 % of the population of Norway attend regular church services held in the Norwegian Church on Sunday morning. However, statistics indicate that about half of the people in Norway believe in God and life after death. There are also several other religious communities that do not belong to the Church of Norway. Many of these arrange religious meetings and conferences in which up to several thousand people participate.

Language

Because settlements were scattered and isolated by mountains and fjords, there are several different dialects in Norway. Two official written languages are used today, "Bokmål" and "Nynorsk". The latter is derived from major rural dialects. "Bokmål" is the language of towns, and has been influenced by Danish (Norway was under Danish rule for more than 400 years). Government institutions such as the Norwegian Broadcasting Corporation, NRK, use a certain percentage of both. The choice of language used in schools is left up to each municipality. In 1994, 17,2 % of Norwegian children attended schools where "Nynorsk" was the official language.

Cities, Towns and Villages

When a population of merely 4.3 million people are dispersed among several urban and agricultural areas, it is easy to understand why Norwegian towns tend to be relatively small. They have developed freely with little planning; the streets in the centre of the community are often narrow and winding, but also full of Nordic charm and attractive details. Only a few buildings from the Middle Ages have been preserved – unfortunately, wooden houses burn well.

There are a great number of towns situated along the coast, often at the mouth of a river, or around a cornerstone industry such as smelting works, shipyards, or fish-processing plants. The towns act as service centres for their own districts, and the government has designated some of them important centres of growth.

From the Bronze Age

Current archaeological investigations of some areas indicate that villages existed during the Bronze Age. Following this era, trading centres and market towns came into existence along the coast. Many of the towns in Western and Northern Norway were based on fishing, shipbuilding and machine industries. Other towns along the southern coast expanded by exporting oak timber to foreign shipbuilders. Soon Norwegians began to build ships themselves, and Norway's fleet of cargo ships became one of the leading merchant navies in the world.

Certain towns like Kongsberg (silver), Røros (copper) and Kirkenes (iron) had their basis in mining activities until the ore was used up and readjustment was essential. Swedish iron ore from the Kiruna district is still exported from Narvik in Northern Norway. Other towns, such as Tromsø, Kristiansund and Ålesund, were founded on islands near shipping routes. The towns of Lillehammer, Kristiansand and Namsos were more or less designated by the government to become important regional centres. Each town has its own history and character.

The capital city has not always been Oslo. Trondheim (the medieval Nidaros) in central Norway was the first capital (from 997), after which Bergen took over. It had become the leading trading city in Western Norway and the largest of all Scandinavian cities.

Later, Oslo became more important because of the industrial revolution in the nineteenth century.

The Sámi people constitute approximately 1 % of the Norwegian population, only 7 % of them are employed in keeping reindeer. They are an ancient indigenous people with their own language and culture. The Sámi people have had a separate popular assembly, Sametinget, since 1989. This functions as an advisory body to the Norwegian authorities in cases concerning the Sámi population. The Sámi Assembly elections are held every four years, concurrent with the general election. The President of Sametinget (2000) is Sven-Roald Nystø.

Oslo – a Melting Pot

Oslo, the country's melting pot, is a city in continuous growth. Including the suburbs, this expansive urban area contains approximately 700,000 inhabitants.

Oslo is an exciting city, with nightlife attractions rivalling most other major European cities. There are many restaurants, nightclubs, theatres, a wide choice of musical performances, museums and films (foreign films are sub-titled).

Embraced by the Oslo fjord to the south and unspoiled natural woodlands to the north and east, the city of Oslo is situated in surroundings unlike that of any major cities.

Bergen, Trondheim and Tromsø all have long traditions of local pride. Stavanger has grown and changed rapidly in recent years, but has managed to preserve some of its beautiful, original wooden architecture.

Tourism

A great number of tourists "discover" Norway every year. In the late 1980s and 1990s tourism exploded.

Fjords, Mountains and Waterfalls

The fjords are traditionally Norway's greatest tourist attraction. The most spectacular scenery is found in the inner inlets of the fjords, often only 500 metres wide with mountains towering on either side. The contrasts between fjords, mountain glaciers, flowering orchards, waterfalls and verdant hamlets have been the source of many themes used by painters and poets, not to mention the composer Edvard Grieg. Surprisingly enough, the climate in the inner fjords is temperate and dry, and there is a considerable amount of fruit production.

Norway is a land of mountains. Its shoreline is deeply carved by the sea, and dotted by thousands of islands. Since the watershed lies far to the west of the country, the rivers in that region are short, with many rapids and waterfalls. Some of them fall several hundred metres into the water. In Eastern and Central Norway, the rivers are longer and the forests are more extensive.

The Norwegian mountains are modest by global standards. The high-

Tourists transported by a Norwegian pony ("fjording") in the mountains of Sogn og Fjordane. In the background, the Briksdal glacier, which is a branch of the famous Jostedal glacier.

Coastal flora in the northwest of Norway.

est of them is Galdhøpiggen, a mere 2,469 metres. However, mountains emerging right out of the water as sheer cliffs or sharp pinnacles have a monumental effect.

The coast of Norway is unique. The Nordland waterway has been dubbed "the most beautiful in the world" by enthusiastic tourists. A myriad of islands stretch out into the sea. On many of them, ice and snow have chiselled out strange rock formations, which have become fairytale figures in the sagas of Northern Norway. In some places, sea-bird colonies cover entire cliffs with thousands of nests.

The valleys are deep, with steep sides. Glittering waterfalls emerge from hanging tributary valleys.

Ships and Churches

Norway did not become a wealthy country until the present century, with industry, shipping and the discovery of oil in the North Sea. Magnificent edifices were not generally built in a poor country with no aristocracy – but there was one exception. Around a thousand years ago, Norway was a great power in Northern Europe, thanks to ship building and maritime skills. During this period, Viking ships and stave churches were built, as well as a number of stone churches. More than 30 stave churches are well preserved and open to the public on the original sites, or at the folk museums in Oslo and Lillehammer.

Many tourists come to Norway by boat. This is the cruise ship SS "Norway" alongside the quay by Akershus Fortress in Oslo.

The finest preserved medieval monuments include the excavated Viking ships in the Viking Ship Museum in Oslo, Nidarosdomen Cathedral in Trondheim, the cathedral in Stavanger and Mariakirken in Bergen.

Rock Carvings

Akershus festning and Bergenhus, the fortresses in the Oslo and Bergen harbours, are architectural treasures from after the reformation. The oldest evidence of human habitation is found on rock carvings (helleristninger) which are found in abundance, some with hundreds of figures. They are found all over the country, maybe most impressively in Alta in the northernmost province of Finnmark.

Other sites of interest include the preserved seventeenth century fortress town Gamlebyen in Fredrikstad, and the mining town, Røros. The same is true of Nusfjord and other fishing villages with picturesque nineteenth century houses in Lofoten. The best collections of Norwegian folk art from this period are found in the Folk Museum in Oslo and Maihaugen in Lillehammer.

Vigeland and Munch

Twentieth century places of interest include the sculpture park created by Gustav Vigeland in the Frogner Park, and the Munch Museum, built to house the paintings and graphic art works of Edvard Munch. These are both in Oslo.

Those who are interested in sports may want to visit the ski-jump and the Ski Museum at Holmenkollen, or the site of the 1994 Winter Olympics; Lillehammer.

Bergen is one of the most distinctive towns in Europe. It is here that Troldhaugen – the home of the composer Edvard Grieg – can be found.

The medieval harbour and the Aquarium, that houses the largest collection of salt water fish in Europe, are also local sites.

There are also great technological achievements to be seen in Norway. Roads wind their way dramatically over the mountains and down to the fjords. The Bergen Railway, with the Flåm line, is very popular with tourists. The same may be said of the bridges spanning sounds and fjords, connecting islands and the mainland.

Tours and other Forms of Vacation

As Norway is known as "Nature's Wonderland", the majority of visitors want to travel around. The sparsely populated country also attracts many visitors who come to enjoy special interest activities.

Touring the country by car is a form of stressless vacationing. Nowhere in Europe do the roads offer better scenery. Traffic safety is very good. Space is abundant. Most running water is drinkable, and the air is "like champagne". Many local communities have their own museum and cultural attractions. A round trip covering an eastern valley through a western fjord district via mountain plateaus can be a spectacular drive. Northern Norway also has good roads, but distances require more sightseeing time.

Special hotel passes are available for motorists offering very favourable rates for a nightstop with breakfast.

Kviknes Hotell in Balestrand in the county of Sogn og Fjordane – a traditional hotel from the childhood of tourism in Norway (built around 1900).

Many tourists believe that polar bears walk the streets in Norway. This is not the case. There are, in fact, no polar bears on the mainland of Norway. However, they are frequently seen on the Norwegian Svalbard islands in the Arctic – and they are very dangerous!

For non-motorists, there is an abundance of offers for bus trips, combined rail/bus routes and special air rates in summer.

There are many special interest activities that can be experienced in Norway. Photography, fishing, birdwatching, mountain hiking, mountain and glacier climbing, and hundreds of museums provide visitors with many opportunities to have an interesting, active and relaxing vacation.

Angling is free in the waters along the coastline, which is longer than the Equator. Thousands of small or large rivers and lakes also offer a chance to catch fish. The further north, the better. There are many salmon and sea trout rivers. In most of these, a licence is required.

Mountain Hikes and Climbing

Mountain hikes can be for anyone. Although not everyone wants to take a strenuous side-trip to the peaks, there are plenty of trails along the mountain plateaus. No other country has such an extensive system, with marked trails that stretch as long as the distance from Oslo to Tokyo. They can be found in all parts of Norway. Along the routes, there are special cabins – some attended, others with self-service – or larger lodges at key points. It's easy to go by car to all routes and park there. The system works from June to September and during the Easter holiday (for cross country-skiing).

Mountain climbing and glacier walking needs some prior knowledge before starting. Courses are offered at several places, especially for glacier walking. Some areas give even the experienced climber challenges.

The Cradle of Skiing

Skiing originated in Norway. Words like ski and slalom come from Norwegian. Ski jumping and slalom competitions started in the county of Telemark.

Today, there are dozens of good winter resorts with thousands of miles of marked trails for cross country skiing as well as lift centres for downhill and slalom. The annual ski festival at Holmenkollen in Oslo attracts a great many participants and tens of thousands of spectators.

Accommodation

In addition to ordinary accommodation, Norway offers a couple of facilities that are unique to the country. There is a large selection of tourist accomodation, ranging from first class hotels to tourist homes, mountain lodges and boarding houses.

Overnight accommodation in rural districts is often run by families who provide an traditional atmosphere, and friendly, personal service. Although Norwegian hotels are not moderately priced, lower inflation in Norway compared with that in other countries in recent years, has made accommodation more affordable than before. During the summer season, hotel chains offer special rates which include passes which entitle the bearer to a one night stop and breakfast for a very reasonable price, and special rates for guests staying more than 3–5 days. Children sharing a room with adults pay half price. Information is available at most tourist information offices around the country.

Many tourists do not sleep in hotel beds, but in a tent, caravan or simple camping cabin at one of the more than 1,100 approved camping sites. These camping cabins are the least expensive and, therefore, the most popular form of overnight accommodation for families.

Altogether, there are 99 "vandrerhjem" or youth hostels (accomodation for hikers) which are suited as well for motorists with families. They often have separate family rooms. The standard is often higher than in many other countries. Youth hostels are open to everyone.

Cottages and "Rorbuer"

Cottages and "rorbuer" are unique to Norway. A vacation at a cottage is the main Norwegian form of recreation in summer as well as winter. Most of the cottages have enough space for many people, so this kind of vacation is reasonably priced for members of a party. The cottage serves as a starting point for mountain walks, boat tours, bathing, berry picking and hunting. They are fully equipped except for bed linen and towels.

Rorbuer (fishermen's cabins) are generally found in Northern Norway, particularly in Lofoten. These were originally used by fishermen for shelter while they fished in the wintertime. Now they are hired out to tourists.

Rorbuer and sea fishing go hand in hand. Boats and fishing gear can be hired at these places. In recent years, a number of tourist apartments and bungalows have been built in Norway.

The restored front of Nidarosdomen, the cathedral of Trondheim. The cathedral was built in the High Middle Ages over the tomb of St. Olav, the king that christianized Norway in the 11th century. Nidarosdomen is the largest medieval building in Scandinavia.

These are generally high standard housing with either full or partial housekeeping.

Restaurants

There is a wide selection of restaurants in larger Norwegian towns, ranging from Italian, French, Spanish, Chinese, and Indonesian to Indian and Thai. There are also restaurants with hamburgers, pizza, hotdogs and, of course, traditional Norwegian cuisine.

When it comes to meat dishes, Norwegian dishes are comparable to the rest of Europe. Lamb is considered to be of the highest quality. The sheep graze on the fresh mountain grass.

Those who really want a typical "Norwegian" meal ought to be on the look-out for seafood restaurants. Norwegian specialities which are internationally known include salmon, sea trout, halibut and cod with melted butter and potatoes. This is best in summer with fresh potatoes. Norwegian delicacies include smoked salmon, trout and mackerel, marinated trout and salmon. For further details about Norwegian food, see pp. 41–44.

Communications and Transport

Travelling to Norway

By Car

A great number of tourists visiting Norway arrive by car. Some, on a round-trip tour of the Nordic countries, enter through Sweden or Finland. Others reach Norway by car-ferry from Denmark, Germany or Great Britain. Drivers meet no practical problems; they may use their own driver's licence, car registration papers and insurance. The average speed limit for Norwegian motorways is between 80 and 90 kilometres (50 and 56 miles) per hour. In developed areas, the speed limit is 50 km (31 miles) per hour, and in certain residential areas, 30 km per hour or less.

By Boat

Several car-ferries arrive daily in Norway. A few of them may be less frequent or even cease running in the winter. There are ferry services from Copenhagen, Fredrikshavn, Hirtshals and Hanstholm in Denmark, from Kiel in Germany, from Amsterdam in the Netherlands, and from Newcastle, Harwich and Lerwick in Great

Travelling by car in Norway, you have to be careful about unexpected obstacles in the road. This friendly encounter takes place at the Sognefjell mountain.

Even in summer, don't be surprised if you happen to meet skiers along the road. This picture is taken early in June at the Trollstigen mountain road.

Britain. In the summer, there are ferries between Norway and the Faroe Islands and Iceland. Tourist Information Centres will assist you in making suitable connections.

By Plane

Norway's most important international airports are Gardermoen in the Oslo area, Flesland in Bergen and Sola near Stavanger. There are direct flights to these airports from a number of European cities. There is also daily service from the USA to Oslo year-round, and to Bergen in the summer. Several regional air connections from other Scandinavian countries and Great Britain are also available.

By Train

Trains arrive to Oslo from Denmark and Sweden daily. Express trains from other European countries come to Norway via Copenhagen or Hamburg. Affordable tickets or train passes are available.

Passports

Foreign nationals from non-Nordic countries must have a valid passport in order to enter Norway and can remain in the country up to three months. Those coming from countries that require a visa, must have their passports stamped at a Norwegian consulate or embassy.

Ninety countries are exempt from the visa requirement, including the United States and Western European countries.

Travelling in Norway

The Railway

The main railway lines branch out from Oslo to the larger towns and cities in Southern Norway and to

Sweden, Denmark and Europe. From Trondheim, the Nordland line continues across the Arctic Circle to Fauske, with a connection to Bodø. Narvik, which lies outside the rest of Norway's railway system, is linked to the Swedish Ofot line. There are connections to Sweden from Trondheim via Storlien and from Oslo via Kongsvinger/Charlottenberg or via Halden/Kornsjø.

In addition to the express and longer routes, the Norwegian State Railway (NSB) provides commuter service and local trains around Oslo, Bergen and Trondheim.

The first Inter City Express (ICE) trains began running at the turn of the year 1992/93. Today, the ICE train routes are Oslo-Halden-Gøteborg (Gothenburg) and Skien–Oslo–Lillehammer–Otta. In addition, there are new express trains running on the Sørlandsbanen (Oslo–Stavanger), Bergensbanen (Oslo–Bergen) and Dovrebanen (Oslo–Trondheim).

Although Norway once had several secondary railway services, many of these have been shut down and replaced by buses in recent years. In areas where there are no railway services, NSB (The Norwegian State Railway) provides bus services.

Travelling by train through the mountainous Norwegian landscape is an exhilarating experience. The highest point on the railway system is on the Bergensbanen between Oslo and Bergen – 1301 metres above sea level. During the journey, the locomotives pull modern comfortable railway cars through mountain tunnels, across bare mountain plateaus and over gorges on impressive bridges. From Myrdal station, the railway line down to Flåm at the Sognefjord has a general elevation of 55 % – one of the steepest railway lines in the world using normal trains – with some breath-taking winding tunnels and, of course, extra braking systems.

The Norwegian railway system extends over 4,012 km (1997), of which more than 2,422 km carries trains that run on electricity. In 1997 40.7 million passengers travelled with NSB and 15 million tons of freight was transported along its lines.

The history of the Norwegian State Railway dates back to 1854, when the first line was opened between Oslo and Eidsvoll. Eidsvoll is where the first Norwegian constitution was written in 1814. Bergensbanen was opened in 1909 after a 14 year-long struggle with challenging topographical conditions in a harsh winter climate with heavy snowfall.

NSB offers various European ticket-passes, for example Interrail, Euro-Domino, Scanrail Pass, Eurail Pass, and Rail Europe Senior. Some of these discounted tickets are only valid for Europeans while others are available to non-European passengers. Tourists over 67 years of age may travel with the Norwegian senior citizen ticket.

Express Bus

An express bus is a pleasant alternative to travelling by train or car. An express bus called Nor-Way Bussekspress covers longer routes in Norway, including more remote areas. In addition, there are also several smaller local bus companies servicing most areas.

Private Vehicles

The roads account for approximately 90 per cent of all passenger traffic in

The world's most beautiful voyage? The Coastal Express (Hurtigruten) has daily departures from Bergen, and calls at 33 harbours on its way to Kirkenes. The tour there and back takes 11 days.

the country whereas sea transportation is responsible for a substantial part of freight transport. There is a high density of vehicles on Norwegian roads. There are 2.5 (Jan. 1998) inhabitants per private car, a number that corresponds to averages in countries like France, Switzerland, Sweden, Italy and Germany. There are, however, relatively few traffic-related problems associated with the density of vehicles, given that there is more road per car and per inhabitant than in any other European country. Immediately following World War II, Norwegian roads were not reputable, but today they meet international standards.

Motorways exist mostly in Eastern Norway, but even the winding roads in the west and north are of acceptable standard. Nearly all national roads and two-thirds of country roads are asphalt.

When driving in Norway, there are three features to take note of. The first is Norway's extensive network of car-ferries. There are 215 scheduled ferry routes operating with remarkable regularity along the Norwegian coastline. The ferries are government subsidised, and fares are established by the authorities.

The second feature, tunnels, facilitate the flow of traffic. Longer tunnels, either through mountains or underwater, substitute ferry service. On some tourist routes, original roads across mountain plateaux are opened during the summer for nostalgic motorists.

The third feature is the building of new bridges across the fjords. These structures are both functional and visually appealing!

Norwegian general policy has given high priority to preserving the country's population structure. One way to obtain this goal is through the development and public investment in regional roads and local infrastructure. Consequently, the cities have had a proportionally small part of the total funds invested for roads.

On state motorways, there are only a few toll stations, and the generated revenue pays for new bridges or tunnels. Around Oslo, Bergen and Trondheim however, there are toll stations set up to finance the construction of main roads and tunnels in metropolitan areas, to minimise air and noise pollution and to improve the efficiency of transportation.

New Route Numbers

Motorists can find several helpful guides and maps that include lists of hotels and ferry timetables. Information pamphlets printed by local tourist offices can be obtained in information centres all over Norway.

Air Traffic

Domestic and international air services are frequent and efficient. With a population of only 4.4 million, Norway is among those countries making the most use of air transport. Over 20 million travellers passed through civilian airports in 1995. In addition, approximately one million travelled to foreign destinations on charter flights.

There are 54 airports, 19 of which belong to the regular network serviced by SAS (Scandinavian Airlines System) and Braathens. SAS is a Scandinavian partnership and is 50 % government owned. The 35 secondary airports are serviced by small planes belonging to regional networks, the largest being Widerøe's Flyveselskap, owned by the Fred Olsen Group.

In recent years, considerable investments have been made in modernising larger airports like Flesland (Bergen) and Sola outside Stavanger. Major investments have also been made at Værnes outside Trondheim. A combined airport/railway system was opened in Værnes in 1994.

Gardermoen Airport

Fifty kilometres north of Oslo, Norway's new main airport, Gardermoen, opened on 8 October 1998. Two runways, new motorways and Norway's first high-speed train will bring 13 million passengers to the airport every year according to all forecasts.

While Oslo's former airport at Fornebu, a few kilometres from the city centre, was congested, the new airport has the capacity to meet the growth in air traffic in the coming years.

Gardermoen's terminal building alone is 137,000 square metres. The airport covers an area of 13 square kilometres, equivalent to 2,000 football fields, and houses 52 plane terminals.

The control tower, a staggering 90 metres, is the second highest in

Distances (km, by road)

Oslo - Kristiansand	329
Oslo - Lillehammer	170
Oslo - Bergen	486
Oslo - Trondheim	496
Oslo - Tromsø	1665
Oslo - Hammerfest	2070
Bergen - Trondheim	651
Bergen - Tromsø	1725
Bergen - Hammerfest	2318
Trondheim - Tromsø	1169
Tromsø - Hammerfest	687
Kristiandsand - Hammerfest	2408

Largest cities
(Population, Jan 1999)

Oslo	502 392
Bergen	227 297
Trondheim	147 150
Stavanger	108 086
Kristiansand	71 481
Fredrikstad	67 423
Tromsø	58 121
Drammen	54 354
(Suburbs not included)	

Railway   Road

NORWAY

dkapp
Mehamn
Berlevåg
Båtsfjord
Vardø
Vadsø
E 6
akselv, Banak
Kirkenes, Høybuktmoen
asjok
Russia
Rørvik, Ryem
Namsos
E 6
Finland
Ørland
TRONDHEIM Værnes
Sweden
Kristiansund, Kvernberget
Støren
Oppdal
Molde, Årøy
Ålesund, Vigra
Åndalsnes
Røros
Ørsta-Volda, Hovden
Dombås
Anda
orø
eland
Sogndal
Fagernes, Leirin
E 6
Lillehammer
Gjøvik
Elverum
Gol
Hamar
Geilo
Gardermoen
Dagali
Hønefoss OSLO
Kongsvinger
GEN
and
Lillestrøm
Notodden
Drammen
Moss
Rygge
und,
Tønsberg
Sarpsborg
Skien
Halden
Geiteryggen
Fredrikstad
Sola
Sandefjord, Torp
Arendal
Flekkefjord
E18
65 km
Lista
Kristiansand, Kjevik

©Chr. Schibsteds Forlag/Hans P. Carlsen

Oslo's new airport, Gardermoen, was opened in October 1998. A high-speed train brings passengers to and from the airport.

Europe. The west runway is 3,600 metres long, and the east 2,950 metres. The airport has the capacity to handle 80 flights per hour or 550 in 24 hours.

The new rail link is the backbone of the shuttle service, and, in conjunction with local and inter-city trains, transports half of all passengers travelling to and from Gardermoen. No other airport in the world has such a high percentage of its passengers arriving by public transport.

The rail link departs from the centre of Oslo and arrives at the train station in the new terminal building on the lower ground floor. The 16 new trains reach speeds of up to 200 km/h along the 48 km route. The train passes through a 13.9 kilometre long tunnel – Romeriksporten, which extends from one of Oslo's suburbs, under forest, water and recreational and residential areas. The train then re-emerges near the town of Lillestrøm. Travel time from Oslo to Gardermoen is 19 minutes. Travellers are met by train personnel wearing uniforms designed by the Norwegian Paris-based fashion designer Per Spook.

Trains depart from NSB Gardermobanen at Oslo Central Station every 10 minutes during morning and afternoon rush hours. In addition, NSB will run local (commuter) trains, inter-city trains and long-distance trains to the airport. The duration of these journeys, however, will exceed 19 minutes.

Gardermoen can also be reached by bus. The airport bus service from the SAS Scandinavia Hotel in Oslo has departures every 15 minutes. Nor-Way Bussekspress, NSB Biltrafikk and Norgesbuss have ten direct routes to the airport from 50 locations in the southeast of Norway.

For those travelling to the airport by car, there are 8,000 parking spaces available at Gardermoen. Four thousand short-term spaces are housed in the multi-storey carpark located next to the terminal building. A corresponding number of long-term parking spaces are approximately 2 kilometres from the terminal building. Shuttle service is available free of charge.

The multi-storey carpark is equipped with a sophisticated, twenty-four hour electronic surveillance system that monitors vacancies on all six floors and displays this information on screens. There is a tunnel from the multi-storey carpark to the terminal building.

Three check-in islands dominate the Departure hall. Each airline company has a clearly marked check-in desk, and television screens provide information about current arrivals and departures.

The security check area acts as a border between the two large office complexes in the hall, and separates the departure hall from the 819 metre wide area allocated to gates. Domestic departure gates are to the left, while international departure gates are to the right.

In most cases, planes arriving at Gardermoen will be accessed by one of 70 covered ramps. Baggage is handled quickly; luggage takes between 3 to 5 minutes to reach the baggage claim area.

The arrival hall includes an information desk for taxis and a ticket office and escalator for NSB trains. Platforms for buses and taxis are outside the arrival hall. Oslo and Akershus taxi companies work in co-operation to provide twenty-four hour taxi service with 140 vehicles.

Culture

Literature

Reading is a very popular acitivity in Norway. According to the Encyclopedia Britannica, Norwegians read more than any other population in the world, spending an average of 500 kroner a year per capita on books. More than 4,000 new titles are published annually in Norway, around 10 % of which are novels, collections of short stories and books of poetry by Norwegian authors.

Looking Back

The most ancient literary remains to be found in Norway are ruinic inscriptions. The powerful heroic and mythological tales and sagas of kings and families originated in the Old Norse period (750–1300). Several of these belong to world literature. Heimskringla, the history of kings, is still a bestseller. Much of the "four hundred years' night" under Danish rule was virtually non-existent in terms of literary production. However, the poet-priest Petter Dass (1647–1707) lived in Norway in the 17th century. The leading literary figure in the Age of Enlightenment was Ludvig Holberg (1684–1754) who wrote poetry, essays and comedies of manners. Henrik Wergeland (1808–1845), possibly the greatest poet Norway has produced, emerged in the years of growing patriotism and national pride in connection with Norwegian independence in 1814.

The second half of the 19th century, with the Nobel Prize laureate Bjørnstjerne Bjørnson (1832–1910) and the world famous playwright Henrik Ibsen (1828–1906) leading the way, is known as "the Golden Age". Knut Hamsun (1859–1952) began his writing career around 1890, followed by Sigrid Undset (1882–1949) and both received Nobel Prizes in 1920 and 1928 respectively. Arne Garborg, Olav Duun, Johan Falkberget, Sigurd Hoel, Tarjei Vesaas and Johan Borgen, as well as the poets Olaf Bull, Herman Wildenvey, Olav Aukrust and Arnulf Øverland, are writers of this century whose books have already become Norwegian "classics".

Present Day Literature

The last few decades have been characterized by an increasing number of female authors, with an emphasis on social criticism rather than psychological studies of individuals, and, especially in the 1970's, political radicalisation. The pendulum began swinging back again in the 1980's with more writers trying to combine elements of social criticism with psychological portrayal.

The rich diversity in Norwegian literature owes a great deal to official cultural policy. One thousand copies of most Norwegian books of fiction, poetry and drama are purchased for distribution to libraries around the country. Many writers have also been

Not many authors can compare his success with what Jostein Gaarder has achieved; 16 million copies of "Sophie's World" has been sold worldwide (spring 1999). Gaarder is here meeting with his Pakistanian publisher.

granted a guaranteed annual income by the Government. Among the best known Norwegian writers today are Axel Jensen, Knut Faldbakken, Kjell Askildsen, Roy Jacobsen, Erik Fosnes Hansen, Herbjørg Wassmo, Karin Fossum, and Bjørg Vik.

Gaarder's Fairy Tale Success

The Norwegian authors of today have also gained recognition outside Norway's borders. Both Faldbakken and Fosnes Hansen have done well abroad, the latter especially so, but even he has not come close to the fairy tale success of Jostein Gaarder during the mid-1990's. His 500-page novel "Sophie's World", aimed at the younger readers, had sold more than 16 million copies by early 1999 and has been turned into a musical and a movie as well. The first part of Fosnes Hansen's 1500-page blockbuster "Tales of Protection" came out in the autumn of 1998, and immediately headed for the bestseller list, which he accomplished with "Psalm at the End of the Voyage", his preceding novel which was loosely based on life on the "Titanic".

Theatre

In Europe, Norway is a newcomer as far as theatrical traditions are concerned. Professional theatre in the capital started as late as 1827, when Johan Peter Strömberg, a Swede, opened his theatre in Oslo (then named Christiania). The oldest existing theatre is Den Nationale Scene in Bergen which has been in operation since 1876. Although the concept of a National Theatre in Oslo did not materialize until 1899, the plays of Ibsen strongly influenced playwrights and theatres all over the world.

Since the 1960's, there has been considerable expansion, with the theatres in Oslo, Stavanger, Bergen and Trondheim establishing subsidiary establishments. In addition, five regional theatres were opened in Tromsø, Mo i Rana, Molde, Førde and Skien. These theatres are based in their respective towns where the theatre groups rehearse and produce plays, and also make extensive tours within their own districts.

Riksteatret, The National Travelling Theatre, was set up in 1948, based on a Swedish model. In Norway and Sweden, the small population is spread over a large area, and economic support given to Norwegian theatres is unique. The central government, as well as local authorities, provide grants covering 80-90 % of the expenses involved in running permanent theatres, without which, such performances would be impossible.

Free Groups

Free theatre groups have flourished in the wake of "the cultural revolution" of the 1960's and include traditional groups or idealistic ensembles given to artistic experiments. These groups have made significant contributions to theatrical activity in Norway. Their first permanent theatre, Black Box, opened in Oslo in 1985. Several smaller theatres of a similar kind have opened in Bergen and Trondheim. However, they often run into economic problems and, far too frequently, end up closing down after only a short time in operation.

Henrik Ibsen

Henrik Ibsen is the most famous of all Norwegian playwrights. At almost any time of the year, at least one of his plays is being performed somewhere in Norway. Plays like "Peer Gynt" and "A Doll's House" are internationally known. Every other year, The National Theatre arranges an Ibsen festival – invariably a great success.

In more recent years, several modern dramatists including Jens Bjørneboe, Finn Carling, Peder W. Cappelen, Edvard Hoem and Cecilie Løveid have made significant contributions. Several Norwegian comedians have enjoyed national film successes and have inspired a variety of comedy stage shows, especially in Oslo. Local stage show activity has also thrived throughout the country in recent years.

Annbjørg Lien is considered as Norway's most talented musician and has been an outstanding ambassador for Norwegian folk music.

Leif Ove Andsnes has attracted considerable interest and excitement since his international career began in the early 1990s. He is now one of Norway's most famous pianists.

Music

Since the 1970's, music life in Norway has changed character. For one thing, working conditions for major orchestras in larger cities have improved noticeably with the building of concert halls. In addition to this, new conductors have revolutionized the quality of Norwegian orchestras in recent years. The best known orchestra outside Norway, the Oslo Philharmonic, is highly respected for its recordings of symphonies of Shostakovich and Tchaikovsky under Mariss Jansons's baton. Several of these recordings have won international prizes.

The Norwegian Chamber Orchestra has also enjoyed international success, and following a guest performance in Paris under the musical direction of Iona Brown from the Academy of St. Martin's in the Field in London, it was acclaimed as being one of the four best chamber orchestras in the world. Another group, the Trondheim Soloists, have also carved

out a place on the world map, and in 1999 made a recording with German violinist Anne Sophie Mutter. Local music schools, funded by local authorities, have become an effective recruiting ground for promising musicians, and among those well on their way into the world elite are pianist Leif Ove Andsnes, cellist Truls Mørk, trumpet player Ole Edvard Antonsen, the Vertavo quartet and the Grieg Trio.

Prominent Opera Stars

There are also many famous Norwegian opera stars. Kirsten Flagstad (1895–1962) has been called "the voice of the century". Ingrid Bjoner is another prominent singer in the Strauss-Wagner tradition. Mezzo-soprano Edith Thallaug, tenor Ragnar Ulfung, bass baritone Knut Skram, and three female stars: Randi Stene, Solveig Kringlebotn and Elisabeth Norberg-Schulz have all appeared on European opera stages, including Milan, Paris and

Vienna. Norway's own operatic tradition dates from as recently as 1959, but in June 1999 Parliament agreed on a proposal concerning the site location of a new modern opera house in Bjørvika. The building will be finished in 2008, and until then the company suffers from having to make do with a theatre building which is not particularly well-suited for opera performances.

Grieg and Nordheim

Edvard Grieg (1843–1907) is undoubtedly the greatest Norwegian composer of all time. Many are familiar with his better known works, such as his piano concerto in A minor from Peer Gynt, his Norwegian Dances and Lyrical Pieces, and Suite from Holberg's time, to name but a few. Harald Sæverud (1897–1992) is the most prominent modern composer of the 20th century, and Arne Nordheim (born in 1931) is becoming even more famous, with his music being performed all over the world. His cello concerto, commissioned by Mstislav Rostropovich, is on the repertoire of many orchestras.

Government Sponsorship

Established cultural activities, music included, are largely financed by the government. In recent years, private sponsorship from leading companies has become more common. Interest in music seems to be increasing. Queen Sonja's International Music Competition, arranged for the first time in 1988, is yet another example of the interest in Norwegian music, both at home and abroad. It generally attracts promising young musicians from all over the world.

Unique Jazz

Norway also has an excellent reputation in the world of jazz music, with several well known musicians and many jazz festivals. The most famous musician is saxophonist Jan Garbarek, whose experimental style has attracted great attention. Bendik Hofseth is a virtuoso on the same instrument, and singers Karin Krog and Laila Dalseth, guitarist Terje Rypdal, bass player Arild Andersen and pianist Morten Gunnar Larsen are all celebrated musicians. The jazz festivals at Molde, Kongsberg, Voss and Oslo, together with the blues festival at Notodden, are visited every year by well known foreign musicians. Mari Boine, of the Sami minority population, has attracted great attention both abroad and in Norway with an unimitable mix of her own nation's music with modern arrangements.

Bel Canto

Since the success of A-ha in the 1980s, Norway has not come up with any really big international pop/rock names, even though groups like Bel Canto have experienced some success. Such groups popular within Norway include Dum Dum Boys, Pogo Pops, Di Derre, DDE, Weld, and Flava To Da Bone. Steinar Albrigtsen, Jørn Hoel and Jonas Fjeld have fans within the the fields of country, roots and pop music. Annbjørg Lien on the Hardanger fiddle has been the most popular of recent folk music artists, often joined by two other musicians in the group De Tre Bukkene Bruse – named after a famous folk tale. Other well known female artists are Anne Grete Preus, Lynni Treekrem, Sissel Kyrkjebø, and Silje Neergaard.

In 1997, the Norwegian film "Søndagsengler" was nominated for an Academy Award in the category best foreign film. From the left: Henriette Engesæth, Marie Theisen (lead) and Ann Kristin Rasmussen in a scene from the film.

Film

Norwegians take an exceptionally great interest in cinema, and most cinema theatres will offer a wide variety of high quality foreign films, although Norway itself produces only a few. Among memorable works in recent history are Arne Schouen's "Gategutter" (Street Boys, 1949) and "Ni liv" (Nine Lives), which received an Oscar nomination in 1957, as did Nils Gaup for his debut "Veiviseren" (The Pathfinder). His story is based on Sami folklore from the Middle Ages, with a script in Sami, Gaup's mother tongue. It also became a great international success, against all odds.

During the first half of the 1980's, the Norwegian film industry was dominated by female directors such as Vibeke Løkkeberg, Anja Breien, and, somewhat later, Bente Erichsen. By the mid-1980's, male directors began to hit the limelight with Ola Solum's "Orion's Belt", an action thriller rooted in Svalbard and international politics, and Leidulv Risan's "Etter Rubicon" (1987). The high technical quality of these films proved that Norwegians were fully capable of making fast moving "American style" action films. This genre was developed throughout the 1990's, and the response from the general public has been very impressive.

Ullmann's Directing Success

The biggest box office success in Norwegian cinemas in 1995 was "Kristin Lavransdatter" based on Sigrid Undset's novel and directed by the well-known actress Liv Ullmann. She also directed "Julia", based on a novel by a Danish author, describing

Jewish life in Copenhagen at the end of the 1800's. Directors such as Marius Holst, Erik Gustavson, Berit Nesheim (who received an Oscar nomination) and Eva Isaksen were noteworthy representatives of Norwegian cinema in the 1990's. Among the more prominent Norwegian actors, we find names such as Espen Skjønberg, Bjørn Floberg, Wenche Foss, Anneke von der Lippe and Kjersti Holmen.

Architecture

The most characteristic feature of Norwegian architecture is the extensive use of wood as a building material. It is still common to build single family houses of wood. The finest expression of wooden architecture in Norway is the stave church, of which there are still around thirty in existence. Having withstood the ravages of wind, rain and snow for between 700 and 800 years, the stave churches are unique in Europe. Norway is the only country in which wooden church architecture was developed to such an extent that medieval churches could be preserved up to the present time. The most important stone church of the period is the cathedral in Trondheim.

With the exception of a few large-scale stone structures such as the Akershus Fortress in Oslo, wood has remained the national building material, and was even used extensively in the innovative and impressive new Oslo Airport at Gardermoen, inaugurated in 1998. Not until Norwegian independence in 1814, with the corresponding need for new buildings, was there much use of stone. Construction then proceeded under the supervision of professional architects, many of whom were foreign nationals. Their place was later taken by Norwegians who had been educated in Germany. The most successful work of this period is the old University of Oslo in the centre of the city, which was completed in collaboration with the great German architect K.F. Schinkel.

Towards the end of the last century, there was a national trend in wooden architecture, with the distinctive "dragon style", inspired by the secular log houses and and the stave churches of the Middle Ages. Henrik Bull's transformation of the international Art Nouveau style at the beginning of the century also reflects national inspiration. The Classicism of the 1920's and the Functionalism (Bauhaus) of the 1930's both gained a foothold in Norway.

Since the war, the focus has been on low structures built close together rather than the blocks of flats that represented former attempts at meeting the need for low-cost housing. The most famous architect of this period is Sverre Fehn (born in 1924), a modernist who was awarded the Pritzker Prize, considered to be the Nobel Prize of architecture, in the mid-1990's. However, he has been given no opportunity to demonstrate his style in Oslo (with the exception of The National School for the Deaf) and his admirers consider him living proof of the difficulty of becoming a prophet in one's own country. His most famous buildings in Norway are the Glacier Museum in Fjærland, and the Aukrust Museum in Alvdal.

Among more recent architectural projects are Aker Brygge in Oslo, Tromsdalen church in Tromsø, and the Hamar Olympic Hall, built for the 1994 Winter Olympics.

Kaupanger Stave Church, built around 1180.

Art

Works of interest within a European context were produced in Norway in the Middle Ages. Frontals, a type of easel painting with a Christ or saint motif used at the front of the altar, were produced in the period 1250–1350. Norway is practically the only country in which these have been preserved. They were painted with oil as a binder around 200 years before the oil technique obtained a real foothold in European painting styles.

There were no first-rate painters in Norway before J.C. Dahl (1788–1857), who became professor in Dresden. His paintings of Norwegian landscapes won him a prominent position among his contemporaries. The next Norwegian painter to win international recognition was Edvard Munch (1863–1944), whose expressive works had an influence on German artists in the early twentieth century. A pioneer in the development of graphic arts as an independent art form, Munch is represented in museum collections all over the world.

During the inter-war years, monumental paintings were produced in Norway that had an influence on art in other Nordic countries. This culminated in the ornamentation of the Oslo Town Hall, done by Per Krogh

Outside urban areas, houses are usually constructed from wood. This is a traditional char-acteristic of Norwegian architecture.

(1889–1965) and other artists. A few of the leading names in Norwegian painting today are Jakob Weidemann, who is an abstract painter, though his works are often inspired by nature; Franz Widerberg, who may be characterized as a figurative expressionist, while Per Kleiva is practically a pop artist. Of the younger generation of painters, Odd Nerdrum is a representative of neo-romanticism.

Sculpture

Gustav Vigeland (1869–1943) was the first Norwegian sculptor to win international renown. His major work is the sculpture park in Oslo, which was named after him. The pioneer of abstract sculpture in Norway was Arnold Haukeland (1920–83), and he was given a number of official commissions. The figurative tradition has been carried on by Nils Aas, while Boge Berg exceeds the boundaries of traditional figurative sculpture. Among the younger sculptors, Gitte Dæhlin is of particular interest with her textile sculptures.

Arts and Crafts

Magnus Berg (1666–1739) had an international reputation as a carver of ivory. There has been a long tradition of wood carving in Norway, beginning with Viking art and the ornamentation of the stave churches, and followed by a highly developed folk ornamentation. The art of weaving is also well developed in Norway. A leading weaver of the day is Synnøve Aurdal, who uses modern materials such as metal and plastic in her tapestries. Norway also has a number of outstanding potters, such as Kari Christensen, and jewellery designers, like Tone Vigeland.

Odd Nerdrum is one of the representatives of neo-romantic painting. Many of his pictures are also sold abroad.

Cultural Policy

Official Norwegian cultural policy is based on a concept of culture that embraces not only the preservation of art and culture, but active participation and individual initiative. Cultural activities in Norway are mainly financed by the public sector, but sponsorship has, in some areas, become more important in recent years. Cultural councils have been set up in almost all counties and local authorities.

Increased Government appropriations have gone towards new buildings and, in particular, greater support for artists. The aim of this is to bring the income level of artists up to that of other groups. The Norwegian artists' associations are the only organisations of their kind with negotiating rights. It is also typical of Norway that institutions receiving considerable Government support are run by the artists themselves.

The Government guarantees a minimum edition for all Norwegian fiction and poetry, and libraries are financed by public funds. Moreover, books are exempt from value added tax. Subsidies are also allocated for printing Norwegian classics and publishing modern drama. In addition, there are funds available to those making their art debut, for the ornamentation of buildings by artists, the commissioning of musical works, the publishing of music and the release of records, and Sami cultural activities.

Museums also receive substantial support, and the Government assists in the preservation of buildings, ships and technological monuments. Much of this support is decentralized and, in addition to this, the Government allo-

"Monoliten" by Gustav Vigeland is probably Norway's best-known sculpture. It is almost 17 meters high and consists of 121 human figures carved in granite. The sculpture is located in Oslo's Vigeland Park.

cate funds throughout the country to theatres, concerts, art galleries, and so on. Norway has regional theatres, regional musicians and municipal music schools, as well as the world's northernmost film group.

Customs

Visiting a Norwegian Home

During your stay in Norway, you might be invited for dinner or to a party in a Norwegian home. As in many other countries, it is a good idea to take along a gift for the hostess (or host if he lives alone) the first time you visit their home. This could be a bouquet of flowers, a box of sweets, or a speciality from your own country. A bottle of wine will also be appreciated. Remember to thank your hostess for the lovely meal, and remark upon her excellent cooking.

One thing that is often strange for foreigners is the custom of taking off your shoes in the hallway when visiting a Norwegian's home. This is for practical reasons, preventing the house from becoming dirty, and primarily concerns boots and winter shoes. If you arrive by taxi, in your best shoes, then, of course, you don't have to worry about taking your shoes off.

In contrast to many other countries, the hostess will not dish up the food, but will usually place each dish on the table so that guests can help themselves. If you are invited for dinner, it will usually be served around 7 p.m.

A "Thank you" for All Seasons

Customs and good behaviour do not only apply to more formal situations. All Norwegian children, from the time they are quite small, are taught never to leave the table after a meal without saying "takk for maten" (thank you for the meal). By learning to say this, a foreign guest will make a very good impression.

If you have an ear for languages, you will perhaps notice another 'thank you' that is very often used, and that is "takk for sist". This greeting, referring to the previous occasion those people spent time together, is typically Norwegian, and can be roughly translated as 'thanks for the last time'. When leaving each other, Norwegians usually say "ha det bra" (have a good time), or just "ha det" for short.

Food – A Feast For The Adventurous

In the larger towns and cities, and particularly in Oslo, you can get the food you are used to eating, no matter where you come from. However, if you are a little adventurous, you ought to let yourself try real Norwegian specialities.

A popular starter is the famous smoked salmon, which is exported world wide. Corned salmon (gravlaks) and half-fermented trout (rakørret) are also Norwegian delicacies.

In most cities you'll find special fish restaurants, some of them really superb, and the waiter will be happy to advise you. A few suggestions for the main dishes are fresh salmon, grilled salmon, halibut, flounder, not to forget catfish. If you happen to be here during Christmas, or in the months of November/December, do try lutefisk.

Lutefisk, dried codfish prepared in potash lye, is extremely popular during the weeks before Christmas. If you have the opportunity to have a real lutefisk meal, we highly recommend it!

This is wind-dried cod prepared in a potash lye. Try to book in advance as some restaurants in Oslo have long waiting lists for a lutefisk meal.

Different parts of the country have their own traditions concerning Christmas dinner. Whilst people in the northern and the southern parts of Norway traditionally eat fresh cod, people in Bergen and the western part of the country enjoy pinnekjøtt, which is the ribs of lamb, smoked and dried. The usual drinks to accompany Christmas dinner are beer and aquavit. Pork ribs and surkål (a kind of sauerkraut) is the typical Christmas meal in eastern parts of Norway. Over the last years it has become more and more common throughout Norway to have turkey for Christmas.

When it comes to lunch, many Norwegians still bring a packed lunch from home, consisting of open sandwiches. The main hot meal of the day, middag (dinner), is eaten at about 5 p.m. in most households. However, visitors who feel it is impossible to change their food habits need not lose heart. Most restaurants and cafés serve both lunch and dinner at continental mealtimes.

Traditional dinners at home include meat cakes, boiled or fried fish, and pork chops, all served with boiled potatoes. However, Norwegians are also gastronomically influenced from all over the world, and dishes such as pizza, pasta and chinese cuisine have now become everyday meals in many homes.

If you get the chance, you should try fårikål, a classical dish of cabbage, mutton and black pepper, and if you hear about a special Norwegian dish called smalahove, get a native to explain. Bon appétit!

Recreation and Fresh Air

Norwegians consider themselves to be outdoor people, climbing in the mountains or skiing at least once a week during the winter. One thing is for sure, the possibilities are unique, both in the countryside and close to the cities. The capital, Oslo, has marvellous surroundings, and hikers and skiers are mostly very friendly and appreciate a chat with foreigners.

The great Norwegian outdoors offers many exciting adventures. Most Norwegians enjoy taking long walks in the forests.

Many Norwegians have their own cabins in the mountains or by the sea and spend many weekends and holidays there. Easter is the most popular skiing holiday. The mountains are also beautiful in the colourful late autumn before the onset of winter.

Enjoy Midsummer's Eve, if you are in Norway on June the 23rd, with bonfires on islands and wharfs, outdoor dances and different activities organized by local communities.

Christmas

Christmas is the most important festival of the year. This is not only because of its religious significance. Since the time of the heathens, the darkest time of the year has been a time for feasting and sacrifice. An orgy of food and drink was believed to mollify the powers of darkness, ensuring the return of the sun.

Preparations are still made weeks in advance in many families. Children have an advent calendar from the 1st of December, and advent candles are lit in the weeks before Christmas. Traditionally, the housewife is expected to make at least seven kinds of pastry or sweet biscuits before Christmas. In the afternoon of the 24th of December, church bells are rung to mark the beginning of Christmas, and many families go to their one and only church service of the year. As in many other countries, Christmas is mostly traditions related to the family, but many parishes arrange joint Christmas dinners and invite people who would otherwise be alone. For nearly 30 years, Oslo has had voluntary arrangements throughout the Christmas period for homeless people and people living alone.

As Norwegians celebrate Christmas Eve, Christmas day is a day for relaxing, but most people have a family dinner, or a late lunch with friends and family.

Opening Hours

In contrast to the strict regulations of earlier days, many food stores do not now close until 10 p.m. during the week and 8 p.m. on Saturdays. Some food stores are also open on Sundays, and most petrol stations, which sell basic supplies, are open 24 hours a day.

Restaurants and bars close at 3 a.m, but some night clubs stay open until 6 a.m. According to a new law, you may now also buy a cognac with your Sunday afternoon coffee.

Festivals

As regards to bank holidays and festivals, Norwegians are blessed by having about ten days off in addition to their four weeks holiday entitlement (five for people past 60), and the extra Gro-dag introduced by our first female prime minister, Gro Harlem Brundtland. The main religious festivals are Christmas, Easter, Whitsun and Ascension Day. In addition, Norwegians celebrate the 1st of May (International Workers' Day), and, of course, the 17th of May (Norwegian Constitution Day). The celebration of the 1814 Constitution is still important to most Norwegians, and the parades with traditional folk costumes, Norwegian flags, brass bands and singing children, is a sight you should not miss if you happen to be in Norway in May.

History

Following glacial recession, Norway became suitable for human habitation. Hunters and gatherers appeared around 9000 B.C. Rock carvings indicate animal husbandry and sea travel between 1500 and 500 B.C. (the Iron Age). More farms were cleared, but they were still supplemented by hunting and fishing. Soon afterwards, invading Germanic tribes appeared, and the coastline up to Troms was permanently settled.

The Viking Period (80–1050 A.D.)

Norwegians had already settled peacefully in Shetland and Orkney, but then around 800 were the first recorded violent Norse invasions which gave the Vikings their bad reputation. In great combined operations, Norwegian Vikings conquered the Isle of Man, the Hebrides, North Scotland and most of Ireland. They also settled in Iceland and Greenland, and, for a short period, in North America (Leiv Eiricsson of Iceland/Greenland). Stories have overshadowed the fact that Vikings were also merchants.

An increase of trade along the coast of Norway created friction among the local chieftains. The first unification was carried out using military force by Harold the Fairhaired around 885. The process continued during the next century, especially by Olav Haraldsson (Saint Olav), who gained a powerful ally in the Catholic church. His death in 1030 set the seal on the work of unification and led to the conversion of the Norwegian people to Christianity.

Greatness and Decline

A period of civil wars, with rivals setting claims to the throne, came to an end in the 13th century, and medieval Norway reached its peak under Håkon Håkonsson. Norwegian dominions were expanded to include parts of the British Isles, Iceland and Greenland. However, the economic and military resources of the country were not sufficient in the long run to maintain control of these far-flung areas. The German Hanseatic towns took over the export and import trade. Norway lost out during the Nordic power

A replica of a viking longship.

struggle in the 14th century, and when 2/3 of the population died in the Black Death, the stage was set for foreign domination.

Danish noblemen controlled Norway, but they could not subdue the Norwegian farmers. Norwegians started sawmills and exported timber, started iron works and built sailing ships. The Norwegian middle class grew in size and influence.

The Year of Revolution

Denmark–Norway fought on the French side during the Napoleonic Wars. The peace treaty in Kiel in 1814 forced the Danish king to cede Norway to Sweden. During this time, Norway declared itself independent, chose a lawmaking assembly and adopted Europe's most liberal constitution. The union with Sweden turned out to be a union with both countries ruled by the Swedish King, but Norway kept its constitutional independence.

The Union with Sweden

During the next hundred years, there were two dominant processes – the political and the economic. On the political side, Norway developed from being a state run by civil servants to a multi-party nation. Under the banner of democracy and equal rights in the Union with Sweden, the Liberal party was victorious and introduced parliamentarism in the 1870s and 1880s.

Around 1840, new industries were introduced and the old industries were expanded. The growth of the merchant navy was immense.

But there was not employment for all. During the next 50 years, 3/4 mil-

lion Norwegians emigrated to North America. Norway exported its social problems and many of her best hands.

Abolition of the Union

Towards the end of the century, the dominant political question was the Union. Norway with its maritime interests demanded its own consular service. The Swedish government refused. Norway put force behind its demands by strengthening its defences, especially the border fortresses.

In 1905, the Norwegian government declared the Union dissolved. In a popular plebiscite, the Norwegian people expressed their preference for a constitutional monarchy, and the Storting (Parliament) unanimously elected a Danish prince, Prince Carl, who as Haakon VII, became King of Norway.

From Agricultural to Industrial Society

In the years following 1905, Norway developed from a mainly agricultural society into an industrial one, partly financed by foreign capital.

In spite of infringements from both Great Britain and Germany, Norway succeeded in its policy of neutrality during the First World War. After the war, Norway gained sovereignty over Svalbard (1925). A while later, Norway also took over Jan Mayen in the Arctic, and Peter I and Bouvet Islands in the Antarctic.

From the beginning, Norway was active in the League of Nations. Fridtjof Nansen's repatriation of prisoners of war and his fight against starvation in Soviet Russia and Armenia partly took place under its auspices.

Celebration of Norway's National Day, May 17th, on Karl Johan street towards the Royal Palace in Oslo.

The economic boom during the war was followed by a depression, which was aggrevated by political instability and minority governments. However, the Labour Party had turned from a revolutionary to a reform party. As a result of the outcome of an agreement with the Farmer's Party to fight the depression, it formed a government in 1935 and introduced a new economic policy. Taxes were increased and public works were started in order to reduce unemployment. Social reforms followed, among them a public pension.

Norway during the Second World War

The march towards a Welfare State was brutally interrupted when Nazi Germany invaded Norway in 1940.

After two months of fighting, the King and the Government fled the country and continued the fight from Great Britain, where The Free Norwegian Armed Forces took part in the allied war effort. An even greater contribution was Norway's merchant navy, which was vital for transporting Allied supplies.

In Norway, the resistance movement carried out intelligence work and sabotage against German installations. 35,000 Norwegians were sent to prisons and concentration camps.

The Post-War Period

The first years after the war were marked by reconstruction. Towns had been bombed, the northern provinces razed to the ground, communications were destroyed, supplies and stocks drained, machinery worn down, and there were large housing shortages.

The next 30 years was a period of continuous growth. The gross national product was tripled. In this process, agriculture, forestry and fishing lost 2/3 of their work force. Industry remained more or less the same, whereas all forms of service work, private and public, expanded greatly. A new transition took place – from an industrial to a service society.

The period also brought a definite establishment of the Welfare State marked by the extension of the National Insurance to comprise a general compulsory pension scheme in 1967. This ensures that all Norwegians are able to secure a decent living if their income fails due to age, sickness, occupational disease or unemployment.

In 1945, Norway was one of the founding members of the United Nations, and the Norwegian foreign minister, Trygve Lie, became its first Secretary General. After the coup in Czechoslovakia in 1948, Norway signed the North Atlantic Treaty and joined NATO. Later, Norway took part in the establishment of the European Free Trade Association (EFTA) and applied for membership in the Common Market.

This, however, led to discord within the parties and among the voters, resulting in an advisory plebiscite in 1972 where a majority of 53.5 % voted against membership.

The Labour government had counted on a yes-majority, so thus was forced to resign.

In 1992, the Norwegian Parliament ratified the EEA (European Economic Area) agreement, negotiated between the 12 EC countries and 7 EFTA countries. The main point of the agreement was that goods, services, capital and persons should have the right to move freely across national borders. This in practice functions as one large market.

Government

The Royal Family

Even though the king today has very little direct political power, a great majority of the population wish to maintain the monarchy. This is due to the great popularity of the Royal Family, and to the fact that they were the nation's symbol of unity during the last war. The Royal Family have been very good ambassadors for Norway internationally, and take an active part in promoting the export of Norwegian goods.

From 1814 to 1905 there was a union between Norway and Sweden – under the Swedish King. When Norway broke away from the union with Sweden in 1905 a Danish prince, Prince Carl, was invited to become Norway's king. He accepted and took the name Haakon VII. King Haakon arrived in Norway in 1905, carrying Crown Prince Olav in his arms.

The Royal Family enjoys a special position in the hearts of the Norwegian people, particularly because of their relentless loyalty to the cause of freedom under German oppression and occupation during the Second World War. The entire country mourned the death of King Haakon in 1957. When his son King Olav V died in January 1991, loyal followers gathered in front of the Royal Palace, placing lighted candles in the snow in his memory.

King Olav's son took over the throne, and was crowned Harald V. King Harald (born 1937) and Queen Sonja (born 1938) were cheered by thousands of jubilant patriots during their coronation journeys along the coasts of southern and northern Norway in 1991 and 1992.

In 1968, while he was still Crown Prince, Harald married Sonja Haraldsen (who was not of royal descent).

King Harald and Queen Sonja, Norway's Royal couple since 1991. The picture was taken in the park outside the Royal Palace.

King Harald and Queen Sonja have two children: Princess Märtha Louise (born 1971) and Crown Prince Haakon Magnus (born 1973).

Government of the People, by the People

All citizens, from the age of 18, have the power to vote. Elections are held every other year, alternating between general elections for Stortinget (The Norwegian Parliament) and local elections for the County Councils and Local Authorities. Parliamentary elections will be held in 2001 and 2005, while Local Authority and county elections will be held in 2003 and 2007.

Stortinget, which has 165 members, is elected for a four-year period. During that period it cannot be dissolved, nor can a new election be called, as is the case in many other countries. Stortinget is divided into twelve standing committees, covering the various main fields of work. In plenary meetings, matters are settled after one reading, however, a different routine is followed with regards to the passing of new legislation. Stortinget is sub-divided into two bodies (houses), Odelstinget and Lagtinget, and bills must be passed by both bodies in succession, and signed by the King, before a law becomes enforceable.

Different counties do not have the same number of representatives, for example, Finnmark has 4 representatives, whereas Oslo has 17.

The Government

In addition to the Prime Minister, the Government consists of 18 ministers. 14 ministers head their own specialist ministries. The Minister of Develop-

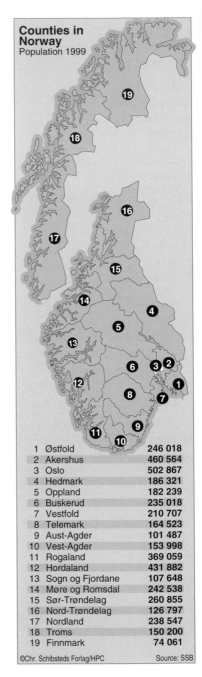

Counties in Norway
Population 1999

1	Østfold	246 018
2	Akershus	460 564
3	Oslo	502 867
4	Hedmark	186 321
5	Oppland	182 239
6	Buskerud	235 018
7	Vestfold	210 707
8	Telemark	164 523
9	Aust-Agder	101 487
10	Vest-Agder	153 998
11	Rogaland	369 059
12	Hordaland	431 882
13	Sogn og Fjordane	107 648
14	Møre og Romsdal	242 538
15	Sør-Trøndelag	260 855
16	Nord-Trøndelag	126 797
17	Nordland	238 547
18	Troms	150 200
19	Finnmark	74 061

©Chr. Schibsteds Forlag/HPC   Source: SSB

ment Cooperation and Human Rights heads a department which comes under the Ministry of Foreign Affairs. Two ministers share The Ministry of Health and Social Affairs – one deals with health matters and the other with social matters.

The ministries are as follows:
– Ministry of Finance
– Ministry of Labour and
  Government Administration
– Ministry of Industry and Trade
– Ministry of Justice
– Ministry of Education, Research
  and Church Affairs
– Ministry of Agriculture
– Ministry of Culture
– Ministry of Environment
– Ministry of Transport and
  Communications
– Ministry of Social Affairs
– Ministry of Fisheries
– Ministry of Defence
– Ministry of Local Government
– Ministry of Children and Family
  Affairs
– Ministry of Foreign Affairs
– Ministry of Petroleum and Energy

Women in Politics

Women are increasingly becoming active participants in the political life of Norway. In 1965, there were only 12 female representatives in Stortinget (Parliament), while women candidates were elected for 60 of the 165 seats in the parliamentary election of 1997. Gro Harlem Brundtland (Labour Party) became the first ever woman Prime Minister in February 1981. Interrupted by different Conservative Cabinets, she also served as Prime Minister from May 1986 to October

1989, and from November 1990 to October 1996.

After the 1997 election, the Christian Democrat Kjell Magne Bondevik became Prime Minister in a coalition cabinet, and 8 of the 19 members of his cabinet are women. The President of Stortinget (Kirsti Kolle Grøndahl) is also a woman.

Political Parties

There are 8 political parties represented in Stortinget for the period 1997–2001. The four largest are Arbeiderpartiet (the Labour Party, 65 seats), Kristelig Folkeparti (the Christian Democratic Party, 25 seats), Fremskrittspartiet (the Progress Party, 25 seats) and Høyre (the Conservative Party, 23 seats).

The others are Senterpartiet (the Center Party, 11 seats), Sosialistisk Venstreparti (the Socialist Left Party, 9 seats), Venstre (the Liberal Party, 6 seats) and Kystpartiet (the Coastal Party) has 1 seat.

County and Local Authority Administration

Norway is divided into 19 counties, including the capital Oslo, which is a separate county. The County Administration serves as a coordinating link between central and local governments.

There are 435 Local Authorities in Norway (March 2000). Each Local Authority collects taxes within boundaries that are prescribed by Stortinget. They are also responsible for schools, social and health services, churches, roads, water, sewerage and electric systems, the fire service, and general planning amongst others.

Education and Research

Education

The Norwegian educational system is divided into primary school (10 years), sixth-form (3–4 years) and university/adult education. All three facets of the Norwegian educational system have undergone extensive reform. A complete restructuring of adult education is being designed.

Most primary schools are state-run and therefore free of cost. The State also maintains institutions of higher education that require students to purchase textbooks and other study materials.

Primary School

Primary schools are compulsory and run by district. They consist of elementary school 1–7, and middle school 8–10. Elementary school is divided into introductory level 1–4 and intermediate level 5–7. In smaller districts, it is not uncommon for children to attend the same school for all ten years of primary education. In cities and larger urban areas, however, there are often separate elementary and middle schools.

In 1969 compulsory education in Norway was increased to nine years, and from the 1997/98 school year to ten years; therefore, children begin at six years of age. The first academic year is a combination of kindergarten and elementary education, and provides a smooth transition to scholastics. With the implementation of ten-year primary school, a new curriculum was also developed. This provides more state control with what students learn, and when they should master each subject. The new curriculum also allows for local adoption and extended use of inter-disciplinary assignments.

Previously, students from non-Protestant families could waive religious instruction based on the tenets of the Norwegian State Church. Now, a mandatory course, which also covers world religions and humanitarian studies, has been implemented. Religious minority groups have strongly opposed this curriculum and have initiated debate concerning its relevance in public primary education.

Natural sciences have been weakened in Norwegian schools, after the creation of a general subject encompassing science, sociology and geography. Attempts at resolving this problem include the introduction of independent science and environmental subjects.

A fundamental principle in Norwegian primary schools is that students are not segregated by ability or proficiency, and grading assessment does not begin until middle school. All children, even those with special needs, are integrated into the classroom. In addition, assistant teachers participate in these classrooms during part or all of academic instruction.

The idea behind the integration or

In accordance with the new reform initiative for Norwegian schools, all students now receive computer training. Most schools however, have encountered economic difficulties in trying to implement this program.

mainstreaming policy is that those with special needs will have other children as role models. In this way, all children are able to interact.

This mainstreaming policy has prevailed for many years, but now criticisms have been raised. Some argue, for example, that individual children with special needs have caused conflict in the school. The critique of the integration policy also points to schools' lack of resources for coping with these children.

English is the principle foreign language that Norwegian school children learn. Beginning in the first scholastic year, students are instructed in English by rhyme and about English grammar rules.

The majority of children in Norway attend state-run schools. Privately operated elementary schools are approved only if they are based on alternative pedagogy or are based on ethical stance. The existing privately operated elementary schools are financed mainly by official funds. Tuition must be at a level where any parent may be able to send their child to these schools.

Sixth-Form Education

After primary school is complete, students may attend Sixth-form College, which lasts three to four years. Normally, students are from sixteen to twenty years of age. These schools are run by district.

Norwegian Sixth-form has academic alternatives. The first, lasting three years, qualifies students for admission to a university or to a technical college. The other alternative allows students to complete a four-year professional education. The last two years of study are designated for apprenticeship. These count as one year of instruction given that one academic year serves as reimbursement to the employer. Professional education ends with a final examination and an advanced craft certificate.

In 1994 extensive reform was carried out in Sixth-form schools especially for professional education. Previously, first year students could choose from over 100 different introductory courses, but now there are only 13 classes available. Each introductory course represents a major subject, but each major still branches into several different tracks after the first year. The reform also implies that all have the privilege, but not the obligation, to obtain three years of Sixth-form education. This privilege must be exercised at some point during the first four years after completing primary school.

Prior to the reform, many began Sixth-form education at a later age. Now, adults are only offered admission after those students completing primary school have accepted admission. The reform inadvertently signifies that many adults are kept out of beginning Sixth-form, although districts are obligated to maintain a certain quota of older students.

The reform has also been criticised because it does not meet the needs of students who are lacking in theoretical knowledge. Moreover, the general introductory courses do not provide students with the same level of competence within their majors as was the case before. The advantage gained however is that students receive a broader education and are better able to change careers if the employment market so demands.

Districts maintain that students are able to pursue the direction of study they desire. This implies that between 90–95 % of students are admitted to the introductory course they prioritise. This does not necessarily mean that the school is properly adapted to general market demands. Many students, therefore, do not obtain apprenticeships, although many positions are available in other branches. Because all students have the right to obtain three-year training, those who do not receive apprenticeships attend a third and final year of Sixth-form college before they take their final examination.

There are a small number of private schools providing Sixth-form education. Authorised schools are financed by public funding and there is a state imposed maximum for tuition. Students who attend unauthorised schools must take exams in all subjects. Tuition covers the costs of running the school and the amount is determined without official guide-lines.

University Education

University education includes universities, science colleges, colleges of the arts and state-run regional colleges. In addition, private colleges offering instruction in mainly economics and computers are included in this category. Colleges and universities are institutions for both research and instruction.

The University of Oslo was founded in 1811 and is Norway's oldest academic institution. There are now also universities in the cities of Bergen, Trondheim and Tromsø. Together with the scientific colleges, these universities have the main responsibility for research and provide research-based instruction and education.

The universities offer three different degrees: cand. mag./Bachelor degree (undergraduate level approx. 4-year study), hovedfag/Master degree (approx. 6-year study) and doctorate/PhD (research degree/study/education). In addition, the universities provide longer professional education within the areas of law, medicine and psychology.

The scientific colleges offer longer professional education in civil engineering, civil architecture, and civil business administration and veterinarian studies. The regional colleges offer mainly shorter professional education from two to four years. The majority of students is concentrated in teacher

The oldest part of The University of Oslo, founded in 1811, is in the city centre. Due to a lack of space, most lectures and courses are held at Blindern, outside the downtown area.

training, engineering and nurse training. Research is also carried out within the regional college system.

The number of students has increased dramatically in the 1990s. Half of all youth in Norway now attend colleges or universities. An improved employment market in the last two years, however, has led to a certain decrease.

Admission to higher education is determined from grades from further education, with a limited possibility for accumulating additional credits from extra courses or work experience. The majority of students are able to pursue the major they desire, and within many subjects, especially engineering, there are several available spaces. In contrast, there is great competition for the most popular majors like medicine, journalism, physiotherapy and civil engineering; grade requisites are demanding. In Norway it is quite difficult to choose applicants on the basis of experience, work tests, entrance exams or interviews. Therefore, grades from Sixth-form are decisive in securing placement in the most popular majors. For this reason, many students spend a lot of money and time in improving grades.

Reform of the regional colleges began the comprehensive education reform in the 1990's. Ninety-eight colleges were merged into twenty-six regional colleges, which means that the majority of Norway's nineteen districts have only one college. With that, the teachers college, nursing college and a number of other subjects were placed under the same school administration. The reform has not yet brought about a reduction in administration costs, a factor that was an original objective.

Adult Education

The possibility of beginning Sixth-form College at an adult age has been an important part of Norwegian education. This possibility, however, is now very limited due to reform in sixth-form colleges.

Nevertheless, adult education is still prevalent in Norway. A large part of adult education is further development for employees in the form of internal company courses, or courses directed by branch organisations. Volunteer organisations have also extensive course offerings that are mainly financed by state funds. Moreover, it is a popular Norwegian hobby to utilise free time in attending different courses arranged by private or district night schools. Course offerings range from ceramics to first level law study. At colleges and universities there is a substantial population of adult students. Some of them receive wages from employers while studying, but most attend refresher courses or continue studies at their own cost.

When unemployment is high, the labour market department has also been involved in extensive re-education initiatives.

Comprehensive adult education reform is now being planned and the objective is that every Norwegian will regularly update education throughout his/her professional career. When adult education has been reformed, the entire Norwegian educational system will have been reformed.

Research

The responsibility for basic research lies with universities and scientific colleges, but more applied research and assigned research are carried out at these institutions. Research is also carried out at the twenty-six regional colleges.

What separates the Norwegian research structure from that of other European countries is mainly the extensive institute sector. A large number of independent research institutes is meant to be the glue between the Norwegian business sector and research sector. These independent institutes receive a small amount of funding from state grants. Income from the Norwegian Research Council, which distributes state research money, contributes to a significant part of research institutes' economic base. For the majority of institutes, however, income from research assignments for industry and from public enterprises is most important.

In 1997 NOK 17 billion was used for research and development projects in Norway. Research for the business sector totalled 7.9 billion while 4.6 billion was used within the institute sector. 4.5 billion was used in colleges and universities. Although as a total this is an increase compared to 1995, research in Norway in 1997 constituted only 1.6 % of GNP in comparison to 1.7 % in 1995. Strong economic growth in Norway in later years has not been matched by corresponding investment in research. This means that Norway uses less of its GNP for research than Sweden, Denmark, Finland, Great Britain, Germany and France. One reason for Norway's position is the extensive utilisation of low technology in the production of raw materials. Large investment in research therefore, is not required.

Norway is not very visible as a research nation, and the Norwegian research sector has barely produced top researchers. The Research Council wants to increase investment in medical and bio-technological research: an objective supported by the Norwegian government.

Defence

The Norwegian Armed Forces function on a compulsory military service basis. During times of crisis or war, Norway is able to mobilise approximately 215,000 soldiers and officers. During peacetime, approximately 18,000 soldiers serve their initial military service each year. In addition to these military conscripts, there are also approximately 11,600 officers and 8,200 civilians employed by the Armed Forces. One of the main problems for all services within the Armed Forces is lack of personnel, especially pilots and technicians. In recent years, many pilots have left and joined civilian airlines. Special agreements, however, providing some groups better conditions and high wages, may solve some of the problems.

Throughout the late 1990s, Norway has been restructuring the peace and wartime roles of its Armed Forces. Efficiency has been increased and peacetime personnel have been reduced. Weaponry, rolling stock, education and training have all been given higher priority.

The objective for the next century is to create a streamline armed force – a force, which through modernisation and an increased use of technology will achieve higher standards. The Defence Budget for 2000 is of 25.530 billion NOK. Similar to the last three years, nevertheless the amount is lower

From the exercise "Strong Resolve" in 1998
(Military's recruitment and public relations centre.)

than expected from the long-term plans in 1992. The budget is 4.1 % of the national budget, and 2.1 % of the GNP. According to the government, the budget will be kept at that level for the next two years. At the beginning of the next century, however, the budget will be raised annually by 0.5 %.

The major equipment programs acquire between 30 and 40 new fighters, up to 6 frigates, up to one thousand new all-terrain vehicles for the army, and a helicopter family intended to meet the needs of all the services.

In order to finance both investment and international obligations within crisis, management and peacekeeping operations, the Armed Forces depend on special grants.

Peacetime Exercises

Despite the fact that Norway has been experiencing a long period of peace, the growing instability and uncertainty in parts of Europe has induced Norway to maintain invasion defence in one area of the country.

The Armed Forces protect Norwegian trade rights and interests. Surveillance and early warning systems are in operation. Norway is also able to support peace keeping operations by having forces standing by.

Initial military service is 12 months, after six months some soldiers, however, will be transferred to the home guard. Here they join local training and exercises, for five to seven days a year as long as they are obliged.

Conscripts who have completed their initial duties normally remain on the military roles until they are 45 years of age. Reserve officers remain on the role until they are 55.

Joint Exercises

Depending on the prioritisation of training and exercises, annual revision training for smaller units and larger exercises with national and allied forces in Norway is carried out.

NATO's Partnership for Peace countries, such as Russia, may participate in joint exercises on Norwegian soil and in Norwegian waters; Exercise Barents Peace in Finnmark 1999. The objective is to co-operate through humanitarian efforts. Mainly due to financial reasons, there will probably be fewer large-scale NATO exercises in Norway.

NATO

Norway is a full member of NATO and belongs to NATO's Northwest Command, which has headquarters in London.

Allied Command South Norway was established in Stavanger in 1994. It is a Principle Subordinate Command, PSC North that includes an international staff consisting of officers from the member states of NATO with particular reinforcement commitments to Norway in case of crisis or war. PSC North is a truly integrated joint tri-service command with a Norwegian commander and with national as well as international duties.

Allied Command North Norway, outside Bodø is both a sub-PSC and a separate national command.

Norway's contribution to NATO's immediate reaction forces (IRF) consists of one infantry battalion (Telemark Battalion) of 900 soldiers, a F-16 fighter-plane squadron and five vessels from the Navy.

Peacekeeping Operations

Norway has adopted an upper limit of 2022 soldiers to aid peacekeeping operations. In 1998 Norway provided the UN and NATO with 800 soldiers for the former Yugoslavia, mainly with SFOR (The Stabilisation Force in Bosnia); and approximately 640 soldiers for the UN-forces in Lebanon. In addition, there are some Norwegian observers in Angola and The Middle East.

Since the UN was founded, Norway has had about 55,000 men and women employed in peacekeeping operations.

In 1997 and 1998, however, there have been recruitment problems. It is more difficult to maintain sufficient and well qualified volunteers for duty. Some efforts have been made through campaigns, but arguments have been raised concerning presence in Lebanon after 20 years serving with UNIFIL.

The Army

During peacetime, the Army consists of 20,000 persons, (including soldiers, officers and civilians), and is able to mobilise 85,000 during wartime.

This branch of the Armed Forces commands one division, six brigades and 20 independent infantry battalions. The main tasks, in addition to contributing to the defence force, are to preserve the Norwegian-Russian border and to be available for international and peacekeeping efforts with the UN and NATO.

The Army's vehicle supply is being modernised. New Leopard (170) tanks are already in place and new armoured infantry combat vehicles, more than 100 CV 9030N, will replace the older ones.

Furthermore, the Army has secured new short-range armoured weapons and a surface-to-surface missile system (NASAMS).

From an exercise at Hjerkinn in 1998
(Military's recruitment and public relations centre.)

The Army is responsible for recruiting personnel for NATO's IRF-force Telemark Battalion. Those who volunteer for the battalion are fully trained one year after their initial service. The training and preparation of UN forces is another of the Army's important tasks.

Since January 1997, a company from Telemark Battalion has been serving with SFOR in Sarajevo. The soldiers are in charge of guarding SFOR Headquarters. At the same time, the company has also been named as SFOR's reaction force in Bosnia.

The Sea Defence

The Sea Defence consists of 3400 soldiers, but is able to mobilise 22,400. It is divided into three groups; the Navy, the Coast Guard and the Coastal Artillery. Their main task is to maintain Norwegian sovereignty, prevent invasion and to carry out escort duties.

The navy has four frigates, 30 MTBs (motor torpedo boats) and 12 submarines, together with mine layers and mine sweepers. Norway is in the process of obtaining new mine assault vessels, and is planning to acquire both new MTBs and new frigates in the coming years. However, the purchase of new submarines and MTBs has been postponed. Although the Navy originally planned to obtain the new frigates within the next ten years, the number obtained may be reduced.

The Coast Guard mainly operates with six vessels, three of the North Cape class with helicopters on board.

The Air Force

The Air Force has approximately 3200 soldiers during peacetime, but is able to mobilise approximately 23,000. Fifty-nine F-16 fighter planes and five F-5s are divided between three main airbases. Norway has not yet decided on a new fighter jet. The fighter force is likely to be cut to four squadrons by 2006.

Norway's future anti-aircraft defence has started to take shape. More than 300 Advance Medium Range Air-to-Air Missiles (AMRAAM) will be used in planes along side the Norwegian Advance Surface-to-Surface Air Missile System (NASAMS).

The main task of this branch of the Armed Forces is surveillance, alert warnings and the control of Norwegian airspace, including with air operations against invasion from the air or sea.

In 1996, Norway withdrew a helicopter unit from Bosnia after having carried out a UN mission for more than two years. Since December 1995, Norway has had three C-130 transport planes working for the NATO Implementation Force (IFOR) from a base in Italy.

Home Guard

The Home Guard was founded following the work of the resistance groups during the second World War. One of its main objectives is to secure the mobilisation of the total defence and to prevent sabotage of military and civilian property. In time of crisis or way, they can mobilise approximately 83,000 men and women.

Foreign Policy

Geography, history and economy are key words for the different factors that have contributed to the formation of Norwegian politics and therefore Norway's relationship to the world.

Geography: Norway is a border state, a small country on the outskirts of Europe. Geographical location has influenced the Norwegian mindset and therefore foreign relations. In a manner similar to that of the British, Norwegians still talk about Europe in such a way that it seems they do not belong to that part of the world.

Both early and recent history has affected contemporary foreign policy. Norway was an old monarchy that later went into union with Denmark and then Sweden. National independence was first gained in 1905. The two world wars in the twentieth century also contributed to the formation of Norwegian foreign policy. While Norway remained neutral during the first World War, the country was occupied by Germany under the second World War. The cold war especially influenced Norway, not only because the country was located geographically between the communist and western worlds.

The Norwegian economy is also important. Norway has always been a nation dependent on foreign countries, maintaining trade relations throughout the world. Since the time when Vikings set off for trading and crusading adventures, the sea has been an international gateway and resource producer. Norway has never been capable of providing a sufficient amount of food for itself, but has exchanged resources for fish and other foods. The situation has not changed after the discovery of oil and gas in the Norwegian coastal shelf in the 1960's, just the opposite is true.

A strong Lutheran tradition with religious missions and feelings of responsibility for the less fortunate have influenced and continue to influence Norwegian politics, manifested in the active promotion of foreign aid and participation in international organizations like the United Nations.

The extensive political upheaval in Europe, beginning in 1989, has also influenced Norway. Because this is a dynamic and continuing process, it is not possible to say what the end-result will be, but the fall of the iron curtain has given both new possibilities and challenges to Norway. This has also provided fuel for a debate about whether foreign policy should concentrate on nearby countries or whether Norway should be globally active as, for example, peace brokers in the Middle East.

North Atlantic Treaty Organization (NATO)

The foundation of Norwegian national security is continued membership in NATO. Norway joined NATO in 1949 due to communist expansion in Eastern Europe and what was then considered a threat from the Soviet. Nevertheless, Norway wanted to have a peaceful relationship with the Soviet

The Nobel Peace Prize is awarded each year in Norway. This picture shows the jubilant Marie-Eve Raguenau from the organization Médecins Sans Frotières, during the 1999 Nobel Peace Prize ceremony in Oslo City Hall, December 10, 1999.

Union and declared its own atomic and military base policies in 1957. No atomic weapons or foreign military bases are permitted on Norwegian soil during peacetime. After the cold war was over, the Norwegian military was restructured and reduced, as done by other NATO members. Norway supports the entrance of new members into the alliance, and actively co-operates with earlier opponents to the Partnership for Peace. OSSE has also been an important instrument in hindering conflict in Europe, and Norway actively promotes this peacekeeping goal.

European Union (EU)

Without doubt, the European Union is the organization that dominates Norwegian foreign relations. In 1972 and 1994 the Norwegian people voted "no" to membership in the EU after the government applied and negotiated a membership agreement. Both times, there was contention between voters for and against membership; the voting population was divided. Arguments ranged from the need to preserve Norwegian independence to economic catastrophe if Norway remained outside the Union. In 1972 53 % voted "no". The Labour party, which then led the Norwegian government and supported membership, relinquished power.

In 1992 the agreement between the European Free Trade Agreement (EFTA) and what was then the European Community (EC) concerning common economic areas was ratified. The European Economic Area (EEA) is still applicable although 52.2 % voted "no" to EU membership on November 28, 1994. Since Denmark, Sweden and Finland are now EU members, Norway's "no" vote to membership has been significant to Nordic co-operation, which has otherwise been close since the Nordic Council was created in 1952. The other Nordic countries look more toward the EU and less to the Nordic countries as a unit. Development in the EU, which is now under expansion, is important for Norway. Today, 76 % of export goes to the EU, while 70 % comes from the EU. Expansion, greater integration and the implementation of a common EU currency, therefore have direct relevance to Norwegian politics.

Neighbouring Countries

Norway wants to include Russia in extensive and constructive co-operation. The objective is to strengthen peace, wellbeing and security in all of Europe and to simultaneously overcome problems resulting from the cold war, especially in northern Europe. Oil and gas co-operation, environmental protection with special emphasis on solving the problem of nuclear waste and nuclear security, expanded trade

Former Prime Minister Gro Harlem Brundtland is now Director General of WHO.

and transport are goals for the co-operation. The Barents region, constituted in 1993, consists of the northernmost districts of Norway, Sweden, Finland and Russia. Co-operation within this region has been continually expanded although there still remains issues unresolved in terms of economics.

United Nations (UN)

Norway participated in the constitution of the UN in 1944–45 and this organization's first general secretary was former foreign minister Trygve Lie (1946–53). All Norwegian governments have emphasised co-operation with the UN and its sub-organizations' work with economic and democratic development. A large portion of Norwegian foreign aid has been distributed through the UN and multinational projects. Norwegian soldiers have participated in UN peace conserving operations (for example, in Lebanon) and Norwegian diplomatic observers have been present after dispute settlements on several occasions.

In 1998 former Prime Minister Gro Harlem Brundtland was elected to the post of Director General of the World Health Organisation (WHO).

Foreign Aid

With the constitution of the Norwegian Government Aid Organization (NORAD) in the 1960's, Norwegian promotion of aid to developing countries increased substantially. Currently, all foreign assistance is co-ordinated by the Directorate for foreign aid (NORAD). The objective is that Norway will give 1 % of GNP in foreign aid. This aid is concentrated on selected countries so that both the giver and receiver have the best exchange of aid.

Oil and Gas

The continental shelf in the North Sea was divided into sectors between coastal states in 1965, before oil was discovered in the region. Norway is not a member of OPEC, but has become an increasingly important actor in the international market. Norwegian companies have also become international. Statoil, for example, participates in Aserbadjan and Nigeria together with other important companies. Internationalisation has also had political relevance; Norwegian foreign policy must take into consideration those countries that may have direct influence on the Norwegian economy.

Perhaps the largest problem Norway currently has with foreign policy is connected to the boundaries of the continental shelf in the Barents Sea with Russia. Since 1970, negotiations have unsuccessfully determined boundaries for an area of 167,000 square kilometres: a possible kingdom for oil and gas. Certain advances have been made, especially after the dissolution of the Soviet Union in 1991. Up to the present, fishing disputes in the Barents Sea, occurring when the economic zone was expanded to 200 nautical miles in 1977, were resolved through a tentative agreement during that same year.

The Judicial System

The Law Courts

The Norwegian Supreme Court, called "Høyesterett", is the highest court of law in Norway. It is composed of a Chief Justice and seventeen permanent justices. In individual cases the Supreme Court sits with a chairman and four judges.

Most cases never get as far as the Supreme Court, but are instead settled in one of the lower law courts.

Previously, for all criminal cases with a prescribed penalty scale of six years imprisonment or more – such as murder, rape, incest, serious narcotics crimes, bank robbery and arson – the court of first instance was the High Court. A jury composed of ten lay-people answered "yes" or "no" to questions of guilt. It was not possible to appeal the decisions of the jury to the Supreme Court, and the possibilities for having a case reopened are extremely limited. This implied that defendants in serious criminal cases could only be tried once on the question of guilt.

New Lawcourt Procedure

On August 1, 1995, a new lawcourt procedure came into effect. As a result, all criminal cases now start in the district court as the court of first instance. Cases are judged by one professional judge and two lay judges, or alternatively, two professional judges and three lay judges.

The Supreme Court building in the city of Oslo.

Oslo's police force changes with the times. In Oslo you can see both bicycle and in-line skate patrols.

Appeals are heard by the High Court which following the reform is an entirely appellant court (Court of Appeal). Appeals can be filed on the grounds of the wrongful application of the law, error in court proceedings, sentencing and judgement of evidence on the question of guilt. It is thereby possible to try the question of guilt twice in all criminal cases. The old jury procedure is maintained for crimes involving a prescribed penalty scale of six years imprisonment or more. If the defendant is found guilty, sentencing is then passed by three judges together with four jury members, who are chosen at random by drawing lots.

Complaints concerning interpretation of the law, court proceedings and sentencing in judgements issued in the High Court, can be appealed to the Supreme Court. Leave to appeal to the Supreme Court must be granted by the Appeals selection commitee of the Supreme Court.

Civil cases

The legal procedures which apply to criminal cases also apply to civil cases. However, the composition of the law court may not always be the same. A civil suit brought before the District court is usually settled by one judge. If one of the parties so wishes, three judges may preside over the proceedings. If the High court is handling a civil suit, there is no jury. Civil cases here are settled by three judges. There may, in addition, be four lay judges if a party so wishes.

The Supreme Court handles appeals from the High Court.

In certain circumstances a case may be heard by the Supreme Court in a plenary session, where all members of the court participate. This may occur, for example, when there is a question of whether or not a law passed by parliament is in accordance with the constitution.

Some Norwegian Acts

Drunken driving

Norway has extremely strict laws concerning drinking and driving, one of the world's most stringent. Routine traffic checks are common. A driver of a motor vehicle with a blood alcohol concentration of more than the allowable limit of 0.05 % can expect severe penalties. A driver with an alcohol percentage between 0.05 and 0.10 will generally receive a suspended jail sentence. If the percentage is between 0.10 and 0.15, the jail sentence may or may not be suspended. A driver with an alcohol content in his blood of 0.15 % or more will usually be imprisoned for a duration of 14 days or more. Penalties also include a larger fine, in addition to a jail sentence. The driver's license of the drunken driver will be confiscated for at least a year, perhaps two. There is talk of lowering the allowable alcohol limit even further.

Narcotics

There are very strict penalties for narcotics violations in Norway. The maximum penalty for such violations is imprisonment for 21 years, which is the longest prison term to which a person can be sentenced in Norway, and is the same as the maximum penalty for premeditated murder.

SUPREME COURT
Rules on questions of principle, including cases concerning interpretation of the law, court proceedings and directives for passing of sentence.

The Supreme Court's Comittee on Appeals
Rules on which cases are to appear for the Supreme Court.

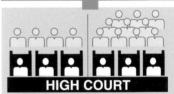

HIGH COURT

2 | **Trial by lay judge court** Most appeals end up here. | **Trial by jury** Appeals where sentence can be more than six years.

HIGH COURT'S «filtering body»
Determines whether less serious cases shall be tried by the High Court.

COURT OF THE SECOND INSTANCE PROCEDURE

1

COUNTY OR STIPENDIARY MAGISTRATE'S COURT
Proceedings for all criminal cases begin here.

 Professional judges

 Lay people

Trial procedure for criminal cases

Trial procedure for serious criminal cases

Social Conditions

Norway is often referred to as a welfare state. Living standards are among the highest in the world, and most people have well-paid jobs. During the beginning of 2000, the unemployment level was a low 3.2 %.

Unemployment levels have also dropped during recent years among the immigrant population. They are, however, the group with the highest unemployment level when compared to the rest of the Norwegian population. At the end of 1999, 6.6 % of ethnic minorities were without work in Norway.

New Family Patterns

During the last century, considerable economic and social changes have affected Norway. The decrease of jobs in agriculture, farming and fishing, for example, has caused workers to migrate from provincial areas to towns and to highly populated districts.

Many people move from the North to the South of Norway, the most popular destination being the capital city of Oslo. Because the majority of people who move are young, the birth rate in regional areas has declined.

The traditional three-generation family unit is becoming less prevalent as an increasing number of marriages end in divorce. However, the divorce rate in Norway is lower than in neighbouring countries, Sweden and Finland. According to the Norwegian Centre for Statistics, two out of five marriages fails within ten years. Oslo has the highest divorce rates in the country.

Divorce statistics, however, do not incorporate the number of common-law marriages that have been dissolved. Common-law marriages, an adult couple living together without any official marriage contract, are an increasingly popular trend in Norway. There are about 500,000 Norwegians involved in common-law marriages, and almost 50 % of all children are born to single parents.

Women and men with newborn babies have the right to paid maternity/paternity leave from their places of employment. They can choose either a full salary paid over a period of 42 weeks or 80 % of salary paid over one year. Similarly, a new father may take paternity leave instead of the mother, a trend that is becoming more common among Norwegian men.

After the period of paid maternity/paternity leave is completed, parents have the right to a one-year leave without salary.

In 1998 the Norwegian Parliament introduced a benefit plan for children from ages 1–3. Parents receive NOK 3,000 monthly if their children do not attend nursery school. The aim is to allow parents to stay at home with their children longer. This policy has created a lot of controversy in Norway. Political critics claim that this is an attempt to keep women away from professional careers. Still, the employment level for women is now higher than ever, and is reaching the employ-

Approximately three out of five Norwegian children age 1–5 are offered placement in kindergarten.

ment level of men in the Norwegian workforce. In addition, the number of working women with young children is also developing substantially. Almost 80 % of women with young children are employed outside the home.

Parents with children under the age of 18 receive an allowance from the state. Single parents receive one extra child allowance in addition to other financial support.

The Norwegian welfare state is based on ideals of equality and justice. Everyone has the right to housing, education, a basic living standard, and health care. The state is also obliged to ensure that everyone can earn a minimum salary base.

Discrimination against anyone on the basis of race, religion, political conviction or sex is prohibited.

Commissioners have been appointed to monitor public administration, sex equality and to advocate children's rights. Considerable sums are filtered through the tax and social security systems in order to re-distribute wealth. The distance between the rich and poor however, is widening.

The National Insurance Scheme

The National Insurance Scheme has replaced all previous private pension schemes as well as government insurance and pension systems. This guarantees everyone minimum retirement pension and disablement benefits, regardless of their economic status. Everyone is entitled to a basic pension, which is inflation adjusted.

The National Insurance Scheme

also compromises the national health system and unemployment insurance.

Public Assistance

Families and individuals who do not have sufficient money for daily living can receive financial support from their county of residence. Public assistance secures them a minimum sum to live on. The allotted sums however, are very low. According to the National Institute for Consumer Research, there are no municipalities in the country which offer social benefits that cover the actual cost of modest living in Norway.

In the 1960s the amount of social clients increased annually, but this statistic has now changed. Since 1994 there has been a sharp decrease in the amount of people receiving benefits. The decline has been largest among younger recipients.

Although fewer people receive public assistance, many still have financial difficulties, especially those who must repay loans. From 1991 to 1996, the sum of delinquent accounts doubled.

In order to aid borrowers in financial difficulty, the Norwegian Parliament introduced the Debt Repayment Policy in 1992 which allows debts to be repaid over a fixed period. The allotted time is usually five years, and debtor must maintain a modest living standard during these years. An increasing number of people

There is a great need for more institutions that can offer care to the increasing number of elderly in Norway.

have to make use of this policy in order to settle outstanding debts.

Health and Social Services

In 1984 the Norwegian government introduced a limit for how much people have to pay for medical and psychological visits and for vital medicines during the year. In 2000 the limit was set at NOK 1,370.

Parliament has also passed a law to ensure that all people who are seriously ill will not have to wait longer than three months to receive care.

Nursing Homes and Convalescent Care Centres

The average age of the Norwegian population is gradually getting older. The amount of people who live past their eightieth birthday will continue to increase well into the next century. Moreover, there are relatively less young people than before. The result of this shift in the population will be that a larger number of elderly people will be supported by a smaller number of young people.

In 1999 there were 188,400 people over 80 years old in Norway. According to forecasts, in the year 2030 the number will be nearly twice as large. Today, the lack of convalescent care centres and nursing homes is a serious problem.

The Parliament has passed an elderly reform which involves extensive expansion of elderly care centres in the coming years. The objective of one reform policy is to ensure all elderly people an individual room at a care centre within year 2001. Currently, 12,000 convalescent care centre and nursing home residents share rooms.

The new reform policies and the expansion of elderly institutions will reduce long waiting lists and create more hospital spaces.

Trade and Industry

At the end of the 1990s and beginning of 2000, Norwegian trade and industry is experiencing a particularly strong growth in the export of goods and services that are not directly connected to the oil industry. During the last twenty years, however, Norway has increased its activity in oil and gas extraction in the North Sea making Norway the second largest exporter of crude oil after Saudi Arabia.

Natural Resources

Norway is unusually rich in energy resources. Not only do the high mountains and great waterfalls provide an ample source of hydroelectric power, but the Norwegian continental shelf contains considerable amounts of crude oil and gas, that has provided an increasing oil production since the middle of the 1970s.

Oil sales throughout the world and natural gas pipelines extending to several European countries have become the largest export business. In 1999, the total export value for oil, natural gas and other petroleum products was at NOK 155 billion. This represents 35 % of the total value of all Norwegian exports.

The significant oil income has provided Norway with profits in foreign

Gas from the Troll A platform in the North Sea flows through pipes into the plant at Kollsnes where the gas is refined and transferred to Europe.

Norway's most important energy source is water. Much of the energy produced is used in power consuming industries.

trade and has given the Norwegian State a considerable annual income. Since 1995, surplus profit from the state budget has been deposited into an oil fund. This money is put into foreign shares, government bonds and other securities. At the end of 1999, NOK 200 billion from the oil fund had been invested abroad. The Norwegian State, represented by the central financial institution Norges Bank, administers the funds as well as the income that goes towards financing pensions and social security.

Exports and Imports

Although oil and gas are Norway's most important exports, the export of goods and services that are not directly related to the oil industry have increased significantly since 1993. In Norway, these goods and services are referred to as the "Mainland Economy" and include all enterprises that

are not connected to offshore activities (oil and gas exploration and production, as well as fisheries and shipping – important Norwegian export industries).

During this period of economic prosperity, beginning in 1993, the annual growth of exported goods has been approximately 8.5 %. In 1998, growth was only 0.5 %, and in 1999 0.6 %. There was a fall in Norwegian exports in 1998 and 1999 due to lower oil prices and to a decreased export of crude oil and natural gas. The increase in exports to countries that are considered as Norway's greatest markets was 6 % each year from 1993–1997. According to the Norwegian Centre for Statistics, Norwegian trade and industry improved its market share during this economic boom.

Norway's ten largest trade partners are the USA, Germany, Sweden, Great Britain, Denmark, Japan, France, Italy, Holland and Spain.

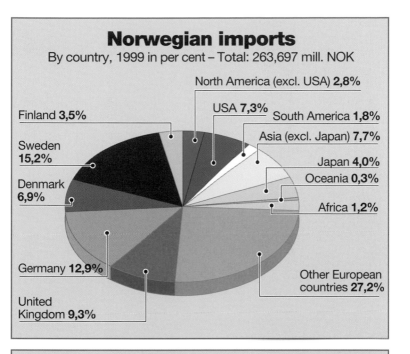

Norwegian imports

By country, 1999 in per cent – Total: 263,697 mill. NOK

North America (excl. USA) **2,8%**

USA **7,3%**

South America **1,8%**

Asia (excl. Japan) **7,7%**

Japan **4,0%**

Oceania **0,3%**

Africa **1,2%**

Finland **3,5%**

Sweden **15,2%**

Denmark **6,9%**

Germany **12,9%**

United Kingdom **9,3%**

Other European countries **27,2%**

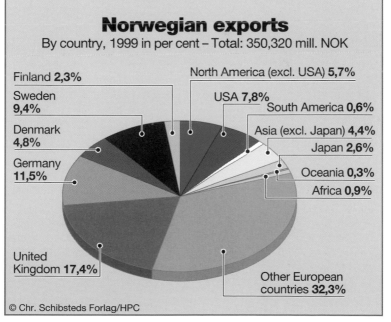

Norwegian exports

By country, 1999 in per cent – Total: 350,320 mill. NOK

Finland **2,3%**

North America (excl. USA) **5,7%**

Sweden **9,4%**

USA **7,8%**

South America **0,6%**

Denmark **4,8%**

Asia (excl. Japan) **4,4%**

Japan **2,6%**

Germany **11,5%**

Oceania **0,3%**

Africa **0,9%**

United Kingdom **17,4%**

Other European countries **32,3%**

Asia is constantly becoming a more important market for the export of Norwegian goods. Calculations from the Norwegian Trade Council, based on data from Statistics Norway, demonstrates that Europe's share of Norwegian export goods has fallen from 82.5 % in 1990, to 76.6 % in 1999. During the same period, Asia's percentage of traditional Norwegian export goods increased from 6.9 %, to 10.5 percent.

Growth has also been registered for exports to North America, South America and Africa. Japan, however, is clearly Norway's largest individual market in Asia and had a total import of NOK 8.4 billion in 1990. Export to China has also doubled during the 1990s, and export to South Korea increased by 424 % according to the Norwegian Trade Council.

Five Important Sectors

The Norwegian Trade Council has chosen to focus its efforts on five sectors within the following investment areas:

* Maritime operations (including the export of shipping, fishing and fish-farming equipment)
* Oil and gas operations (with emphasis on off-shore activities)
* Foodstuff (including fish and agricultural products)
* Electricity (including hydro-power

Norway is among the largest fishing nations in the world, and the fisheries are the country's second largest export industry.

plants, power distributions and the Energy Economy project ENØK)
• Military repurchase

Norwegian trade and industry delegations have participated in various official visits often headed by King Harald, Queen Sonja and leading politicians representing the investment countries. According to the Norwegian Trade Council, official visits and delegations are considered an increasingly important strategy for trade and industry profiling and for the cultivation of high-level business contacts.

Agriculture

A country like Norway with its mountainous regions, cold climate and remote settlements is far from ideal for agriculture. The growing season varies in length from 190 days in the south to just 100 days in the north.

Due to these factors and a political desire to maintain settlement in these areas, a number of agricultural subsidies are available. (However, these have been proportionally reduced over recent years.) The total number of farms has fallen from approximately 200,000 in 1950 to around 77,400 in 1998. Nevertheless almost 10 % of the population is still employed in farming or in related industries.

Milk production is the cornerstone of Norwegian agriculture. 347,200 cows between 24,100 farmers produced over 1,650 million litres of milk in 1999 – a litre per day for every Norwegian. Besides this, Norwegian farmers produce 213,300 tons of meat, 46,940 tons of eggs, 1.4 million tons of grain and 435,000 tons of potatoes yearly. Forestry activites fell between 8 and 12 million cubic metres of timber each year.

Norway's unique climate also possesses certain advantages. For example, because of the slow growth and ripening, Norwegian berries and fruit are extraordinarily tasty. The export of these quality products is on the constant increase. The cold climate also reduces parasite and pest problems in crops, and thereby reduces the need for pesticides etc.

The use of hormones and similar growth stimulants for animal breeding is forbidden under Norwegian law.

Fisheries

The export of fish and fish products increased 15 % from 1997 to 1998, worth NOK 28.3 billion in 1998. 59 % of exports went to EU countries. Salmon exports totalled NOK 7.6 billion in 1997. This is 31 % of the value of all Norwegian fish export. France and Denmark have been the most important importers of farmed salmon for many years. Salmon export to the USA has declined markedly since 1990 due to high import tolls on fish goods. Export to Japan, in contrast, has increased considerably.

The export of fish and fish products accounted for 8.5 % of all exports in 1998.

The 100 largest Norwegian export companies

Here, export consists of each company's collective sales outside Norway – both in export sales from Norway and sales from any activities abroad. Local production abroad is also included in the export figures.

		Export 1998
Rank	*Company name*	*NOK 1.000*
1	Den norske stats oljeselskap a.s	92.666.000
2	Norsk Hydro ASA	88.940.000
3	Kværner ASA	68.132.000
4	Asea Brown Boveri AS	20.751.000
5	Aker RGI ASA	19.167.000
6	Orkla ASA	16.745.000
7	Norske Skogindustrier AS	12.097.000
8	Hydro Aluminium ASA	12.087.000
9	Dyno ASA	10.681.000
10	Elkem ASA	9.100.000
11	Saga Petroleum ASA	6.500.000
12	Merkantildata ASA	6.009.000
13	Wilh. Wilhelmsen ASA	5.849.728
14	NCL Holding ASA	5.786.400
15	Elf Petroleum Norge AS	5.757.628
16	Norske Conoco AS	4.899.145
17	Star Shipping AS	4.705.254
18	Fina Exploration S C A	4.467.600
19	Rieber & Søn ASA	4.303.158
20	Norway Seafoods ASA	4.211.273
21	Telenor AS	4.183.000
22	Tiedemanns – Joh. H. Andresen ANS	4.048.000
23	Mobil Exploration Norway Inc.	4.028.335
24	AL Industrier AS	3.918.640
25	Leif Høegh & Co. ASA	3.811.000

Rank	Company name	Export 1998 NOK 1.000
26	Odfjell ASA	3.787.745
27	Ulstein Holding ASA	3.180.600
28	Jotun AS	3.032.772
29	BP Norge UA	3.017.130
30	Kverneland ASA	2.994.000
31	Borregaard Industries Limited Norge	2.918.058
32	Kongsberg Gruppen ASA	2.810.000
33	Nera ASA	2.628.000
34	Unitor ASA	2.500.000
35	Tinfos AS	2.428.500
36	Scancem International ANS	2.369.111
37	Norsk Agip AS	2.238.558
38	Total Norge AS	2.133.062
39	M. Peterson & Søn AS	2.121.000
40	Det Søndenfjelds-Norske Damskibsselskab	2.120.000
41	Raufoss ASA	2.096.630
42	DNHS Seafoods AS	1.860.000
43	Domstein ASA	1.710.000
44	Tomra Systems ASA	1.695.000
45	Ericsson AS	1.660.000
46	Lerøy Seafood Group ASA	1.640.608
47	Smedvig ASA	1.591.000
48	Ask Proxima ASA	1.534.913
49	Elkjøp ASA	1.531.700
50	Fesil ASA	1.520.000

Rank	Company name	Export 1998 NOK 1.000
51	Fundia Bygg AS	1.512.467
52	Fosen Mek.Verksteder AS	1.299.266
53	Norzink AS	1.271.000
54	Hydralift ASA	1.230.000
55	Narvesen ASA	1.205.000
56	Rwe-Dea Norge AS	1.202.880
57	Alcatel STK ASA	1.200.000
58	Actinor Shipping ASA	1.170.000
59	Scana Industrier ASA	1.161.800
60	Amerada Hess Norge AS	1.114.269
61	Global Fish AS	1.083.048
62	Enterprise Oil Norge Limited	1.073.452
63	Helly Hansen ASA	1.056.000
64	Tandberg Data ASA	985.505
65	I.M. Skaugen ASA	979.000
66	Aker Brattvaag	860.000
67	Glamox AS	850.000
68	Siemens AS	840.000
69	Ekornes ASA	810.800
70	AS Olivin	792.555
71	Kverneland Klepp AS	790.000
72	Selmer ASA	790.000
73	Lai Berg Holding AS	765.500
74	Jakob Hatteland Holding AS	764.400
75	Jordan AS	748.000

Rank	Company name	Export 1998 NOK 1.000
76	Volvo Aero Norge AS	740.000
77	Kavli Holding AS	735.676
78	Arcade Drilling AS	734.871
79	C. Tybring-Gjedde ASA	730.000
80	Pan Fish ASA	652.000
81	SE Labels ASA	650.000
82	Fundia Profiler AS	640.698
83	Sjøvik AS	636.330
84	Kongsberg Simrad AS	630.000
85	Navia ASA	628.269
86	Jangaard Export AS	625.000
87	Kongsberg Offshore AS	616.000
88	Alcatel Telecom Norway AS	601.000
89	TINE Norske Meierier BA	601.000
90	Hunsfos Fabrikker ASA	600.472
91	AS Aalesundfisk	600.000
92	Alcatel Kabel Norge AS	587.000
93	ABB Miljø AS	567.883
94	Hitec ASA	550.000
95	Bjølvefossen ASA	525.000
96	Luxo ASA	518.876
97	Veidekke ASA	514.000
98	Stormbull AS	513.000
99	Varner-Gruppen AS	506.400
100	Eltek ASA	489.500

Source: "Norges største bedrifter", 33. edition, Økonomisk Literatur Norge A/S

Norwegian export companies – Top 10

1   **Den norske stats oljeselskap a.s**

Export 1998:   NOK 92.666.000.000

Statoil, owned by the Norwegian state, is one of the world's largest net sellers of crude oil, and a substantial supplier of natural gas to Europe.

2   **Norsk Hydro ASA**

Export 1998:   NOK 88.940.000.000

The publicly owned industrial compagny Hydro operates in mineral fertilizer, industrial chemicals, oil and gas, hydroelectric power, aluminium, magnesium and plastic raw materials.

3   **Kværner ASA**

Export 1998:   NOK 68.132.000.000

Kværner is an Anglo-Norwegian group, specialising in technology-based engineering, manufacturing and construction services for a wide range of industries.

Asea Brown Boveri AS

Export 1998: NOK 20.751.000.000

ABB has played a prominent role for more than a century in the development of Norway's energy resources and manufacturing. ABB is a powerhouse for technology, research and development.

 Aker RGI ASA

Export 1998: NOK 19.167.000.000

Aker RGI is an active industrial holding company, but also undertakes financial investments. Main investments are currently in oil and gas technology and seafood consumer products.

 Orkla ASA

Export 1998: NOK 16.745.000.000

Orkla's core business areas are branded consumer goods, chemicals and financial investments. Orkla mainly operates in the Nordic countries and in Eastern Europe.

 Norske Skogindustrier AS

Export 1998: NOK 12.097.000.000

Norske Skog is an international forest industry group and one of the world's leading suppliers of printing paper, with production in Norway, Austria and the Czech Republic.

❽   Hydro Aluminium ASA

Export 1998:   NOK 12.087.000.000

Hydro Aluminium Extrusion is a leading manufactur-
er of extruded aluminium products, with plants in all major markets in
Europe and the Americas and is engaged in international joint ventures
in Asia and South Africa.

❾   Dyno ASA

Export 1998:   NOK 10.681.000.000

Dyno is a Norwegian owned international commercial explosives and
speciality chemicals corporation, with operations in over 40 countries
around the world.

❿   Elkem ASA

Export 1998:   NOK 9.100.000.000

Elkem is a leading supplier of metals and materials. Main products are
ferroalloys, silicon metal, aluminium and microsilica.

Norwegian Export Companies – in alphabetical order

ABB Miljø AS

ABB Miljø develops and supplies purification and recycling systems to industrial and offshore operations, and ventilation and air-conditioning products to commercial and institutional buildings.

Aker Brattvaag

Aker Brattvaag is an internationally leading shipyard corporation consisting of six companies. Aker Brattvaag has constructed and supplied shipping vessels and offshore-, supply- and specialised vessels.

AL Industrier AS

A.L. Industrier AS

Alpharma Inc. is a speciality pharmaceutical company with global leadership positions in products for humans and animals. Alpharma is presently active in more than 60 countries.

Alcatel STK ASA

Alcatel STK works within the development of telecommunications and the supply of energy in Norway, and has installed cable and telecommunication systems in nearly all parts of the globe.

Amerada Hess Norge AS

Amerada Hess Norge, a wholly owned subsidiary of Amerada Hess Corporation (New York), has been active on the Norwegian continental shelf since 1965 and has been a substantial producer of oil & gas since 1982.

Ask Proxima ASA

ASK Proxima develops and manufactures data and video projectors for a worldwide market.

Bjølvefossen ASA

Bjølvefossen ASA, located in Ålvik Hardanger, is the world's largest producer of ferrosiliconmagnesium.

Borregaard Industries Limited Norge

Borregaard is a chemicals company with 20 production units in 12 countries. The company has 2,600 employees. Borregaard is a member of the Orkla Group, one of Norway's largest companies.

Det Søndenfjelds-Norske Damskibsselskab

Det Søndenfjelds-Norske Damskibsselskab (DSND) supplies subsea installation and maintenance work for the world's offshore industry.

Domstein ASA

Activities and operations include fish-farming, fishing vessels and fish processing. Domstein's main markets are countries in the EU, Eastern Europe, Southeast Asia and Japan.

Ekornes ASA

Ekornes ASA, manufacturer of the world famous Stressless recliner, is currently Scandinavia's largest furniture manufacturer.

Ericsson AS

Ericsson supplies tele- and data-communication products to the Norwegian and international markets, and operates extensive industrial activities in Norway.

Elf Petroleum Norge AS

Elf Petroleum Norge AS is a subsidiary of Elf Aquitaine, and the principal business is gas production and exploration.

Fesil ASA

The Fesil Group is a major producer of silicon metal and ferrosilicon. The group has three plants, all of them in Norway: Holla Metall, Lilleby Metall and Rana Metall.

Elkjøp ASA

The Elkjøp Group is a trading company in the field of consumer electronics and household electrical appliances.

Fosen Mek. Verksteder AS

Fosen Mek. Verksteder (FMV) is a medium sized shipbuilding company located in Rissa, Norway, specializing in building RO/RO vessels and RO/RO passenger vessels.

Eltek ASA

The Eltek Group's business includes development, production and sale on the world market of power supply systems and fire protection systems.

Fundia Bygg AS

Fundia Bygg is a manufacturer of armoured products with its main markets in the Nordic countries and Northern Europe. Fundia Bygg is Norway's largest recycling company.

Enterprise Oil Norge Limited

Enterprise Oil is one of the world's leading independent oil exploration and production companies. Our business is to provide shareholders with capital and income growth through the discovery, development and acquisition of oil and gas reserves.

Fundia Profiler AS

Fundia is one of Europe's leading manufacturers of long steel products. The products are manufactured in Norway, Sweden and Finland. There are sales and further processing companies on a number of European markets.

Glamox AS

Glamox is a supplier of lighting and electrical heating products to the professional market, including the marine sector and offshore petroleum-installations.

I.M. Skaugen ASA

 I.M. SKAUGEN

The I.M. Skaugen Group is engaged in marine transportation of petrochemical gases, LPG and organic chemicals, as well as ship to ship transfer of crude oil.

Global Fish AS

Global Fish AS Enterprises is a producer of pelagic fish for comsuption. Global Fish, Ottofish and Skaarfish are all brands in Global Fish AS Enterprises.

Jakob Hatteland Holding AS

The Hatteland Group deals with import and distribution of electronic components and industrial monitors in the Nordic countries and the Baltic States.

Helly Hansen ASA

Helly Hansen is a leading manufacturer of high performance outdoor clothing and an internationally well know brand within sport/leisure and workwear.

Jordan AS

Jordan is a Norwegian family company with 200 years traditions in brush making, oral care and painting tools. Jordan has more than 1.000 employees in manufacturing and marketing organisations located all over the world.

Hitec ASA

Hitec was established in 1985 as a supplier of automation and control systems solutions to the oil and gas industry, and has become a world leader in high technology.

Jotun AS

Norwegian based Jotun is an international producer of paints, coatings, varnish and powder coatings. The Jotun Group has 34 factories in Europe, Middle East, Asia/Pacific and Africa.

Kavli Holding AS

Kavli Holding, established in 1893, export cheese spreads, natural crispbread and fresh Norwegian caviar to more than 40 countries world wide.

Hydralift ASA

Hydralift is a worldwide supplier of equipment to the oil- and gas industry and the shipping industry.

Kongsberg Gruppen ASA

KONGSBERG

Kongsberg Gruppen is one of Norway's foremost high-technology corporations. The Group has two main business areas: Kongsberg Maritime and Kongsberg Defence & Aerospace.

Lai Berg Holding AS

Kenmore KMP and Virginia KMP are international trademarks within the global refrigeration and air-conditioning industries.

Kongsberg Offshore AS

Kongsberg Offshore is the world's leading supplier of systems for the extraction of oil and gas on the seafloor and for the measurement of oil and gas.

Leif Høegh & Co. ASA

Leif Høegh & Co is engaged in the transportation of gas, dry bulk, forest products, cars and trailers; in the liner and reefer trade and in ship management.

Kongsberg Simrad AS

Kongsberg Simrad AS is a high-tech company specialising in marine electronics. The company operates globally, with products and services in two main market areas: offshore and ocean survey.

Lerøy Seafood Group ASA

Lerøy is a supplier of seafood from Norwegian waters: whole or value-added salmon, trout, white fish and pelagic fish in fresh or frozen condition.

Kverneland ASA

Kverneland is a leading producer of farm implements with production companies in Norway, Denmark, England, Germany, The Netherlands, Italy and France.

Luxo ASA

Luxo is a supplier of lighting at workplaces in offices, industry and health segments. Geographical markets include Europe, North America, the Far East and the Pacific.

Kverneland Klepp AS

Kverneland Klepp is part of Kverneland ASA, known as the world's leading plough maker.

Merkantildata ASA

Merkantildata is a leading supplier and integrator of information- and communication technology in Nordic countries. The company has offices in Norway, Sweden, Denmark and Finland.

Mobil Exploration Norway Inc.

The oil company Mobil is an active partner in several licensed operations and development projects on the Norwegian continental shelf, like Statfjord, Oseberg, Njord, Åsgård and Kristin.

Norsk Agip AS

Norsk Agip is a fully-owned subsidiary of the Italian company ENI S.p.A, and is active in oil and gas exploration and production on the Norwegian continental shelf.

Narvesen ASA

Narvesen is divided into four business areas: Retailing Norway, Retailing Sweden, Wholesaling and Catering.

Norske Conoco AS

Norske Conoco is a large oil and gas producer in Norway. Conoco, celebrating its 125th anniversary, is a major, integrated energy company based in USA and active in 40 countries.

Navia ASA

NAVIA AVIATION

Navia Aviation supplies instruments for air traffic operations: Instrument landing systems, flight inspection systems, voice switching systems and air traffic control systems.

Norway Seafoods ASA

Norway Seafoods is a vertically integrated food processing company within the entire value chain of seafood products. Aker RGI Holding maintains a 100 % equity share of the company.

NCL Holding ASA

Norwegian Cruise Line operates cruise lines in the Caribbean, Bermuda, the Panama Canal, Alaska, Europe, South America and Australia. In February 2000, NCL was acquired by the Asian company Star Cruises.

Norzink AS

Norzink is located on the West coast of Norway. Main products are zinc and aluminium fluoride for the Western European market.

Nera ASA

Nera develops, manufactures and sells telecommunications equipment and systems. Main products are microwave radiorelay systems and mobilesatellite communication systems.

Odfjell ASA

Odfjell is a specialist in transportation and storage of bulk chemicals, acids, vegetable oils and petroleum products.

A/S Olivin

A/S Olivin, owned by the Norwegian state, has the world's largest known deposit of high-quality olivine and is the world's largest manufacturer of olivine sand products for the international iron and steel industry and other applications.

Rwe-Dea Norge AS

Rwe-Dea Norge AS (former Deminex) has played an active part on the Norwegian Continental Shelf as partner on production licences for more than 25 years and as operator of one exploration licence since 1991.

Pan Fish ASA

Pan Fish ASA, listed at Oslo Stock Exchange, is one of the world's largest producers of farmed raised Atlantic salmon, selling its products of fresh and value added salmon to all major seafood markets world wide.

Saga Petroleum ASA

Saga Petroleum is a large upstream oil and gas company, founded in 1972 to coordinate Norwegian industry's participation in the oil business.

M. Peterson & Søn AS

Peterson Group, with head office in Moss and production i Norway, Finland, Sweden and Denmark, is a global supplier of virgin fibre based packaging materials and applications. Peterson is one of the largest family owned companies in Norway.

Scana Industrier ASA

Scana is an industrial group within materials technology, marine equipment and offshore services & equipment.

Raufoss ASA

Raufoss, established in 1896, is 50.3 % owned by the Norwegian Government. Business areas are commercial vehicle industry, water and gas distribution, defence, composite products, forming technology (parts for personal car).

Scancem International ANS

Scancem International is one of the leading global companies in the cement production and trading area. The business area's main markets are located in the United States, Africa, eastern Europe and Asia.

Rieber & Søn ASA

Rieber & Søn is one of Norway's leading industrial groups, with activities in the business areas foods, packaging, roads and other activities. The main markets are the Nordic region and Central Europe.

SE Labels ASA

SE Labels is Europe's largest manufacturer and supplier of self-adhesive labels.

Selmer ASA

The main business is execution of contracts for building and civil engineering projects, but in addition Selmer works within niches in the building market through specialist companies.

Tandberg Data ASA

Tandberg Data supplies digital information storage solutions for network systems. Subsidiaries are located in USA, Germany, France, UK, Singapore and Japan.

Siemens AS

The electrotechnical company Siemens has got export sales within the fields of energy, telecommunications, shipping, offshore and electrical heating to countries all over the world.

Telenor AS

 Telenor

Telenor is a public limited company wholly owned by the Norwegian state, and is Norway's market leader in the field of telecommunications, data services and media distribution.

Smedvig ASA

Smedvig is an offshore drilling contractor. The company provides services within well construction and reservoir and well technology.

Tiedemanns – Joh. H. Andresen ANS

Tiedemanns is a privately owned industrial group, with extensive finance and investment activities in addition to a wide range of production companies.

Star Shipping AS

Star Shipping is an international marketing and operating company specialising in open hatch vessels designed for transportation of unitized cargoes and containers.

TINE Norske Meierier BA

The dairy co-operative TINE Norwegian Dairies is owned by 25.000 milk producers. TINE exports more than 25.000 tons of cheese every year. The most important markets are Japan and USA.

Stormbull AS

Stormbull AS is a privately owned investment and management company that, through active ownership, secures added value.

Tinfos AS

Tinfos Papirfabrik, a cardboard and paper mill founded in 1875, utilised the power from the waterfall for nearly one hundred years. The power is still utilised within Tinfos but now in the production of metallurgical products.

Tomra Systems ASA

Tomra is a provider of reverse vending machines and solutions for recovering used beverage containers for recycling or reuse.

Veidekke ASA

Veidekke has a diverse portfolio of operations in the building, heavy construction, industrial and property sectors, operating primarily in the Norwegian market.

Ulstein Holding ASA

Ulstein Holding designs and produces ships and maritime equipment for the international market. The corporation consists of 38 companies in 17 countries.

Volvo Aero Norge AS

Volvo Aero Norge AS

Volvo Aero Norge is a leading manufacturer of critical components for commercial and military jet engines and commercial gas turbines in the European and American market.

Unitor ASA

Unitor is an international group which supplies technical products and service to the international merchant fleet and shipbuilding industry. Our products are distributed via a worldwide network, operating in a total of over 75 countries.

Wilh. Wilhelmsen ASA

Wilhelmsen Lines

The company is involved in many activites in the maritime sector. Wilhelmsen Lines is one of the world's leading operators of Ro/Ro's and car carriers. Wilship handles the company's transactions of tankers, bulk carriers and bunkers.

Varner-Gruppen AS

The men's clothing chain, Dressmann, is the cornerstone of the entrepreneurial concept in the Varner-Gruppen. The majority of the stores are located in Norway and Sweden.

AS Aalesundfisk

Aalesundfisk is a consortium of 15 companies. They are engaged in the catching, rearing, processing, sales and distribution. The main markets are Norway, Denmark, France and Chile.

Economy

Norway has enjoyed a period of prosperity and strong economic growth since 1993. In 1999 the Norwegian economy was at a turning point after a considerable amount of instability nationally and internationally during 1998.

The rise started after extreme unrest within the exchange market in Europe in the autumn of 1992 and was superseded by a marked fall in interest rates. The lowering of interest rates was the main factor behind the upswing in the market. The boom resulted from lower oil prices and a particularly Norwegian price level that was out of rhythm with trade partners. The imbalance in the economy led to pressure on the Norwegian crown and in 1998 the Norwegian Central Bank was forced to repeatedly increase interest rates. Since 1999, interest rates have been gradually reduced.

In the spring of 1999, the Centre for Statistics stated: "The Norwegian economy is in imbalance, but far from debilitated".

Apart from oil activity and shipping, economic growth in mainland Norway was approximately 25 % from 1990 to 1999. Growth in the mainland economy was at 3.3 % in 1998 and 0.8 % in 1999.

The economic boom in the late 1990s has been succeeded by a period of reduced growth. Nevertheless, high pressure on selected segments of the Norwegian economy continued at the turn of the century, especially in the labour market where a lack of qualified personnel affected many sectors and industries.

At the beginning of 2000, Norges Bank issued new estimates that assessed economic growth for the period 2000-2003 at between 1.7-2.2 % annually. Norges Bank anticipated a slight increase in unemployment from 3.2 % in 1999 to 4 % at the beginning of the 2000s, and declining inflation from 2.2 % in 1999 to 2 % in 2003.

Norway has an open economy, where 37 % of the total domestic demand is met by imports, while 40 % of added value is exported. Norway is strongly influenced therefore, by present trends in the international economy, especially in Europe and in the USA.

Added value, measured in the gross national product (GNP), was NOK 1189.3 million in 1999. The annual growth in 1999 was 0.8 % for the total economy and 3.5 % for the mainland economy (excluding oil and shipping). This indicates that Norway experienced economic growth lower than the averages reported in its trade partners (2.5 %) and EU countries (3.5 %).

Wages, Prices and Labour Market

The long-lasting economic boom has not resulted in an increase of prices above the norm although the shortage of skilled manpower in 1998 created an underlying pressure to increase wages and prices. Since 1997, growth in the price of consumer goods has fluctuated between 2–2.5 %. This is almost twice the price growth as registered with trade partners and with countries that have introduced the Euro currency where price increases in 1998 were at 1.2 %.

Since 1993, the economic upturn has led to greatly improved employment figures. From 1988–1992, Norway experienced the worst levels of unemployment since the second World War, reaching an all time high of 140,000 (5.5 %) in the winter of 1992/93. Employment levels increased to 235,000 (11.6 %) from 1993 to 1998, while the unemployment rate was more than halved. In 1998, 59,500 (3.2 %) were registered as fully unemployed as opposed to an average of 4.1 % in 1997.

The total workforce in Norway is nearly 2.3 million people. In 1999, the number of active workers (both self-employed and employees) in the age group of 16–67 was 73.2 % of a total population of 4.4 million. This is the highest working percentage ever registered in Norway. According to economists, this indicates that Norway has a marginal work force reserve and a substantial growth in employment must occur by importing manpower from other countries, first and foremost from the neighbouring Nordic countries.

The heavy demand of employment in recent years has put pressure on the labour market. An increase in the demand for skilled workers has created a shortage of specialists. The worst problems have been in finding manpower in industry, the building and construction industry, the health and social sector and within the fast growing information technology branch (IT).

After several years of slight increases in wages and bonuses, the shortage of manpower has exerted pressure on wages, manifesting itself in the annual wage negotiations introduced in spring 1998. The wage increase in 1998 was at 6.25 % and in 1999 at 5 %, while the average wage increases from 1993–97 were at 3.5 %. Wage increases for Norway's most important trading partners in the last few years have been significantly lower (3.3 % on average). Industry fears that it will lose the ability to compete if the increase in wages and the wage level is essentially higher in Norway than in competing countries.

Wages are fixed partly through central and local negotiations in individual companies. Generally, this two-part system applies to industry, but wages for large groups employed in the public sector (national and municipal) are negotiated centrally where they also negotiate a sum to be divided between the different branches.

There are four national organizations for employees. The largest in Norway is Landsorganisasjonen (LO) with over 800,000 members. Akademikernes Fellesorganisajonen (AF) has 120,000 members, and Yrkesorganisjonenes Sentralforbund (YS) has 240,000 members. A division in AF was created when several membership associations and member groups resigned and created a main amalgamation, Akademikerne, which has 111,000 members. Other large national interest organizations related to labour are Norway's Farmers' Association (Bondelaget), Norway's Farmers' and Small Farmers' Association (Norsk Bonde- og Småbrukarlag) and Norway's Fishing Association (Norges Fiskarlag) which is an amalgamation of all trade and industry interests in the fishing sector. Næringslivets Hovedorganisajon (NHO), the main organisation for employers, consists of 15,500 businesses comprised of over 450,000 jobs. Another large employers' organization is Handels- og Service-næringens Hovedorganisasjon (HSH) with 9500 member companiees and a total of 250,000 employees. In total, there are 626,000 employment positions in the service and trade sector.

Significant economic growth, low interest rates, low price increases and moderate growth in wages and salaries have given wage earners an annual disposable income growth (growth in income minus price increases) from 0.5 to 2 % since 1993. This has stimulated private demand and increased private consumption. The growth in private consumption, which was at 1.8 % in 1998 and 1.2 % in 1999, was one of the most important driving forces behind Norway's economic prosperity in the late 1990s.

Low interest rates and income growth have increased loans from banks and other financial institutions. The change came during the second half of 1998 when interest rates increased significantly and demands for loans, especially for private persons, fell. Profit and high prices for property sustained growth in consumer spending.

Business and Industry

Gross national product (GNP). Divided according to industry

	Added values	Employ- ment	Investment in fixed capital	Export- value
Public administration (state and local auth.)	17 %	29 %	16 %	–
Industry and mining	14 %	16 %	10 %	40 %
Oil activity	19 %	1 %	27 %	39 %
Private services	47 %	49 %	43 %	19 %
Primary industries (farming and forestry, fisheries)	3 %	5 %	4 %	2 %

Source: Centre for Statistics 1994

A characteristic of the Norwegian economy is the oil sector's large share of the GNP. Norway is a young oil country. It started with the discovery of gas in Groeningen in The Netherlands in 1959. This led to geological interest in the possible existence of petroleum in the North Sea. The first exploration permit for boring and extraction of oil and gas in the Norwegian section of the Continental Shelf was given in 1965, and exploratory drilling was carried out in the summer of 1966. The discovery of oil and gas was first made in 1967 (The Balder Field). However, it was in the autumn of 1969 that the American Oil Company, Phillips Petroleum Company, made its largest discovery in the Norwegian shelf in the North Sea, the Ekofisk Field. Since

Oslo børs – The Oslo Stock Exchange

then, there have been a series of dis-
coveries in the North Sea, the
Norwegian Sea north of the 62nd
parallel and in the Barents Sea.

Oil production in the Norwegian
shelf commenced in 1971. With the
extractable oil and gas reserves discovered so far, Norway has the resources
to produce oil for 14 years and gas for
approximately 80 years at the present
level of production.

In 1999, the daily production level
in the Norwegian shelf was on average
3.3 million barrels of crude oil (1 bar-
rel = 159 litres). Norway is the world's
6th largest oil producer and the
world's second largest oil exporter.
The export value through the sale
of oil and gas amounted to NOK
123 billion in 1998. This constituted
29.8 % of Norwegian export.

Another energy resource significant
for production, employment and
added value in the Norwegian economy is hydroelectric power. Hydroelectric power production constitutes
3.4 % of added value (GNP) in mainland Norway. In comparison, oil production constitutes 11.8 % of the total

added value in the entire Norwegian
economy.

A large proportion of hydroelectric
power is used by industry, especially
the large smelting works in the aluminium in the ferro-alloy industries.
Price and tax reductions are given to
companies using hydroelectric power.
These government subsidies contribute to keeping cost levels down.

Industry in Norway accounts for a
relatively low proportion of employment when compared with other
industrialised countries and it is particularly energy-based. In the course
of the last 24 years, employment in
industry has been reduced by 100,000
man-labour years.

Norway is among the largest fishing
nations in the world. The fisheries are
the country's second largest export
industry. In 1998, the volume of fish
exported from Norway had a total
value of NOK 26.2 billion. The volume of export remained nearly
unchanged from the previous year.
There has been a continuing rise in
the export of farmed fish in the last 20
years where the demand for salmon is

Fiscal Budget 2000

(Revenues in the fiscal budget including social security)

Revenue	NOK million	Expenditure	NOK million
Taxes on property and income	92 961	The monarchy	168
Duties on employer and national insurance	117 527	Government	116
Customs revenue	1 817	The Norwegian Parliament	781
Value added tax	115 100	Supreme Court	45
Excise duties on on alcoholic beverages	8 521	Ministry of Foreign Affairs	13 216
Excise duties on tobacco	7 380	Ministry of Church, Education and Research	24 723
Tax on motor vehicles	29 148	Ministry of Culture	3 554
Other special excise duties	17 818	Ministry of Justice	10 742
Income under ministries	18 978	Ministry of Social Affairs	28 667
Interests from government enterprises	3 367	Ministry for Children and Family Affairs	23 061
Interests on cash holdings and claims	9 060	Ministry of Fisheries	1 947
Dividends	3 454	Ministry of Transport and Communication	17 372
Repayment	45 404	Ministry of the Environment	2 610
		Ministry of Government and Regional	60 271
Income from state petroleum activity	70 450	Ministry of Administration	17 050
Taxes and duties on extraction of petroleum	35 100	Ministry of Finance	23 193
		Ministry of Agriculture	14 989
		Ministry of Defence	25 530
		Ministry of Oil and Energy	1 272
		Ministry of Trade and Industry	4 046
State petroleum fund	13 282	Other Expenditure	5 607
Transfer from the national bank	10 685	State banks	59 417
Other incomes	16 373	Government petroleum activities	20 530
		Government services	2 491
		Social security	169 909
		Government petroleum fund	85 120
Total revenue	616 427	Total expenditure	616 427

particularly high in the large markets. The largest markets for Norwegian fish exports include the EU, USA and Japan.

Employment growth has mainly occurred in the public and private service sectors where total employment has increased from 65 % in 1970 to 74 % in 1999. The largest growth in employment has been within the public sector, especially in health and care work in local authorities.

The Finance Industry

In the last 10–15 years, the finance industry has undergone a total transformation from a highly regulated credit system to deregulation, free competition and large technological changes.

The fall in oil prices during 1985–86 and the subsequent depression led to a banking and financial crisis where the three largest private banks – Den norske Bank (DnB), Christiania Bank and Kreditkasse (Kreditkassen), and Focus Bank suffered unprecedented financial losses. In 1991–1992, the Government took control in order to safeguard accounts and maintain the trust of international capital markets in the Norwegian banking system. Private investor shares in the banks were lost. In 1992, the country's largest insurance company, Storebrand, lost its equity capital after an unsuccessful bid to take over the Swedish insurance company Skandia. The insurance company was supplied with new private capital while the values of former stockholder shares were set at zero.

Following the economic boom of 1993, the large banks were again declared "healthy" and have gradually been refloated by the raising of private capital through share issues. Fokus Bank once again became a private, regional bank for mid-Norway in 1995. The government's controlling interest in DnB and Kreditkassen has been gradually reduced by 50 % through share issues. The parliament (Stortinget) has decided that the government's controlling interest in the two banks will be reduced to 1/3. In the spring of 1998, preparation began for large-scale privatisation of the two banks through the sale of shares.

The banking system in Norway is divided into commercial banks, savings banks and national banks. In 1997, the 28 Norwegian and foreign commercial banks and credit enterprises (including the national bank, Postbanken) had joint total assets of NOK 613 billion and the 133 Norwegian savings banks had joint total assets of NOK 370 billion.

The national banks provide loans, subsidies and securities for specific groups, industries or sectors. Institutions providing loans include: Statens Lånekasse for utdanning (education), Landbruksbanken (agriculture and forestry), Statens nærings- og distriktsutviklingsfond (venture capital for trade and industry), Husbanken (house-building), Kommunalbanken (financing and investing in local authorities and county councils), and Postbanken (personal and business ventures, competing on equal terms with commercial and savings banks).

In recent years, there has been a gradual change within the finance sector, where banks, insurance companies and other financial institutions cooperate to provide all types of financial services. This development, with transnational mergers and takeovers, has been accelerated by economic and monetary union within the EU and the introduction of a common currency from 1999. Although Norway is not a member of the EU, Norwegian financial institutions are strongly influenced by developments in Europe. Consequently, Norway's largest bank, DnB, took over the country's second largest insurance company, Vital, in 1997 and Kreditkassen has taken over the insurance company Norske Liv.

Norway's third largest commercial bank, Fokus Bank, was acquired by Den Danske Bank in 1999. DnB acquired the Government owned Postbanken in 1999. The Governmental ownership in DnB increased therefore, from approx. 51 % to approx. 60 %.

Swedish-Finish MeritaNordbanken's bid on the acquisition of Norway's second largest commercial bank, Kreditkassen (Christiania Bank & Kreditkasse), triggered political proceedings with the objective to secure national ownership and control in at least one of the three large financial institutions (DnB, Kreditkassen and the finance/insurance corporation Storebrand). The Parliament assigned the Government's investment fund (the Government's holding company in DnB and Kreditkassen) to outline possible solutions. There are several possible alternatives: merger between DnB and Kreditkassen; merger between DnB and Storebrand; merger between Kreditkassen and Storebrand; or the conglomeration of all three large financial corporations in one company. Resolution regarding this issue is expected in the second half of 2000.

A number of credit enterprises obtain funds through debentures. They provide long-term financing, e.g., of private and business properties and ships. Commercial banks are joint owners of "Eksportfinans". They are also a number of finance companies providing specific credit services, inter alia, factoring, leasing, hire purchase contracts and credit cards. The larger of these companies are owned by banks and insurance companies.

Tax and Public Finances

The tax level in Norway is among one of the highest in Western, industrialised countries that are members of the Organisation for Economic Co-operation and Development (OECD). In 1998, tax contributions made up 43.1 % of GNP.

Individual taxpayers pay a flat rate of 21 % to local authorities and counties. In addition, each taxpayer pays 9.75 % in income tax to central government. Government tax is a graduated tax for income over NOK 277,800 per year (tax bracket 1) and NOK 329,000 (tax bracket 2). For income over NOK 762,700 there is an extra tax of 19.5 %. In addition, each individual taxpayer pays 7.8 % of gross income in National Insurance to public pensions, savings and social security scheme. Private taxation is divided into two brackets: tax bracket 1 for individuals without family deductions, and tax bracket 2 for taxpayers with family deductions. An additional capital tax is paid (up to 0.5 %) for net worth over NOK 500,000. Independent of income amount, interest income and other financial income is taxed at a flat rate of 28 %.

In 1998, the government's total revenue increased by 7.1 % from the previous year to NOK 471 billion. The local authorities' total revenue increased 3.8 % (NOK 188 billion).

Due to oil profits, Norway has a surplus in both international trade and within government budgets. The government accounts for 1997 revealed a surplus of NOK 70 billion. Because of lower oil prices and production, the Government predicts that the surplus will be NOK 34 billion in 1998.

The government's substantial annual surpluses have been allocated to an "oil fund" that will finance future pensions from the pension scheme. The fund's money is placed in foreign stock and other securities. The annual return can be used to make up the current deficit (excl. oil revenue) in the annual budget. At the first half of 1999 capital in the oil fund was NOK 182.7 billion. NOK 73 billion was placed in shares, NOK 109 billion in bonds. In 1998, returns were at 12.86 % on the share portfolio and 9.31 % on the bond portfolio.

In addition to tax, duties and direct profits from oil activity, the government's largest source of revenue is value added tax on the sale of goods, which will contribute NOK 115 billion to the Treasury in 1999. Income and property tax from individuals account for only NOK 87 billion of the government's total revenue. Other profits to the treasury include duty on cars and petrol (NOK 29 billion), tobacco (NOK 7 billion) and alcohol (NOK 9 billion).

A substantial portion of the government's total revenue is transferred to individuals and industries as government subsidies. The largest sum (NOK 190 billion) is allocated to pensions and social security benefits from the social security department. The local council sector received NOK 82 billion, farming was allocated NOK 12 billion and NOK 157 billion went in direct subsidies, loans and guarantees to private trade and industry.

The Norwegian Central Bank was founded in 1816. Its main functions are: issue of banknotes and coins; to be the government's adviser regarding money, credit and foreign exchange matters; conduct public information schemes and promote effective systems of settlement and administer the "oil fund". The government appoints the Board of Directors as well as the Head (since 1999 Svein Gjedrem) and Deputy Head (since 1996 Jarle Bergo).

The exchange rate for the Norwegian crown has been connected to the ECU since 1990 and is a weighted average of the currencies in EU countries. Since 1999, the exchange rate is tied to the Euro. Previously, the crown were tied to a basket of currencies, which included the American dollar and the Japanese yen. The crown left this basket in favour of European currencies. In connection with the extensive unrest within the currency market in Europe in the autumn of 1992, the Norwegian crown was "let loose" and moves freely with fluctuations between the ECU currencies. The Norwegian Central Bank's goal is to maintain a stable rate for the crown, measured against the ECU. In the spring of 1998, Norwegian authorities decided that financial and currency policies will be directed towards ensuring stability in the value of the crown against the European currencies when the common monetary unit, Euro, is introduced.

A large portion of Norway's foreign trade, especially the sale of oil, gas and shipping, is settled in American dollars. The value of the Norwegian crown in relation to the US dollar has increased in the last few years from an average of

NOK 7 for one American dollar in 1993–1994, NOK 6.58 in May 1996, and NOK 7.15 on average for 1997, to NOK 7.55 in 1998 and NOK 7.80 in 1999.

The Stock Market

The Oslo Stock Exchange, founded in 1818, is the only market that trades in shares, bonds and other financial instruments in Norway. In total, there are 216 companies registered with the Stock Exchange, the largest, Norsk Hydro, being partially state run and having a market value of NOK 83 billion (as of February 2000). According to the Stock Exchange, total market value of the companies was NOK 512 billion at the end of 1999, in increase of 45 % from the previous year. The total turnover of share profits amounted to NOK 446 billion in 1999, an increase of 38 % from the previous year. The total index rose 46 % in 1999 and was 1359.6 points at the end of the year (1983=100). Foreign ventures listed with the Stock Exchange are approximately 31 % and have remained at this level for the last few years.

Mass Media

Television and Radio

Norway's dramatic landscape, with tall mountains and deep valleys, makes broadcasting difficult. The Norwegian National Broadcasting Company (NRK), therefore, is the only television broadcasting company that has nation-wide coverage. Although the amount of Norwegian and international radio and television channels have increased rapidly in recent years, many Norwegians still have just one television channel: NRK1.

NRK was established in 1933 – the same year the broadcasting law was passed in Norway. At that time, trial radio broadcasts were already being carried out by private companies. Television broadcasts were made permanent in 1960. Before then, only NRK radio offered media coverage. During the second World War, all radio receivers were seized by German occupational forces. During this period, BBC radio

news was the only news coverage Norwegians could receive, and even then only from hidden receivers.

In 1984, NRK established its second radio station, the culture channel "P2", and it was at this time that the first privately owned local radio stations appeared. Nine years later, NRK established its third radio station, the youth channel "Petre". Today, over 48 % of all listeners tune in to NRK radio. The main channel, NRK P1 alone, is responsible for 37 %, Petre 11 % and P2 6 %. Other competing stations include the commercial success P4, and the urban channel Radio 1.

NRK has always been a leader in the radio sector, and in digital radio (Digital Audio Broadcasting). In 1998 NRK established Europe's first digital radio channel. NRK News Only is radio's equivalent to CNN International, broadcasting both national and international news twenty-four hours a day. During that same year, NRK

Harald Heide Steen and Rolv Wesenlund. Together, these two men are "Wesensteen" and they have entertained Norwegians for many years on NRK television. Wesenlund also has his own talk show on the commercial channel TVNorway.

introduced the digital channel NRK Always Classic. For more than fifty years, NRK monopolised Norwegian broadcasting, similar to BBC in Great Britain. In 1992, authorities allowed commercial television broadcasting, and in the autumn of 1992, TV2 was established, financed partially by advertisement. TV3 and TVNorway (TVNorge) had already been established, but were only distributed via cable and satellite.

The Norwegian National Broadcast Company (NRK) was a governmental foundation until 1996. Today, NRK is a public limited company completely owned by the state. NRK broadcasts both on radio and television. The station is mainly financed by licensing fees collected from viewers, and the Managing Director for NRK is employed by the Norwegian government.

In 1996, NRK established a second channel, NRK2. Presently, NRK2 does not have the same amount of coverage as NRK1, and has not been widely successful in terms of viewer numbers.

NRK1 is Norway's largest television channel. TV2, the second largest, has become a commercial success in spite of the difficulties the station encountered during its initial phase. The prosperity of TV2 is attributable to its focus on news, sports and popular series. TV2's operating profits for 1997 were NOK 155 million. In addition, the station obtained 49.3 % of TVNorway's shares – a company struggling with a large deficit. TV2 has therefore established a monopoly on television advertisements in Norway. In 1997, the revenue from television advertisements in Norway amounted to NOK 1.8 billion.

Today, 82 % of the Norwegian population can view TVNorway.

Comparatively, NRK1 is available to 100 % of the population, TV2 to 95 %, NRK2 to 74 %, and TV3 to 59 %. In addition to this, local stations have broadcasted in Norway for many years. The progress of these local stations results from re-organisation, initiated by the authorities in 1996. During that same year, TVNorway established a national network of local television stations. Up to this point in time, this has not been economically successful. Several small commercial stations (niche channels) have also entered the market. More often than not, however, these channels quickly disappear.

More recently, the number of international television channels have rapidly increased, due to the popularity of cable and satellite equipment. Today, almost 300,000 Norwegians possess satellite receivers. In addition to this, digital television, the latest wave of technology in the world of mass media, was established in Norway in the autumn of 1998, by the French/Norwegian company Canal Digital Norge.

Newspapers

Today, Norway is among the leading nations globally in terms of newspaper distribution, issuing approximately 2.962 million copies daily. Nine out of ten Norwegians read a newspaper each day. Moreover, it is quite common for Norwegians to subscribe to a smaller local newspaper. In addition, most read either a national or regional newspaper.

There are a total of 220 newspapers in Norway. Approximately half of the "secondary newspapers" receive operational support from the government. The amount of support offered, however, decreases annually, putting smaller, local papers at risk of bankruptcy.

Norwegian soap operas have become very popular. Henriette Lien, Toralv Maurstad and Beate Eriksen star in TV2's long-running series "Hotel Caesar"

Previously, Norwegian newspapers were politically biased, and largely used as a political sounding board. Nowadays, however, the majority have declared themselves to be politically independent.

Three large media corporations mainly control Norway's newspaper market: Orkla, Schibsted and A-press. Together, these corporations control 66 % of Norway's daily press. Verdens Gang (VG) has the largest circulation and Aftenposten has the second largest, with two daily editions. The media corporation Schibsted owns both VG and Aftenposten. This company also owns TV2 and the Swedish newspaper Aftonbladet. Dagbladet, a tabloid newspaper, has the third largest circulation and is distributed throughout Norway. All three papers have daily publications – including Saturdays and Sundays.

Magazines

Norwegians are also among the leading nations in terms of the distribution of magazines. In 1997, 4.2 million international magazines were sold in Norway. On average, Norwegians spend 189 minutes daily watching television, 151 minutes listening to the radio, 56 minutes reading newspapers, 12 minutes reading magazines, 8 minutes scanning the Internet and 4 minutes reading technical or professional magazines. In the country's capital, Oslo, each inhabitant reads, on average, two magazines regularly. The number of international magazines sold in Norway has increased considerably. In 1998 approximately 1300 different magazines were sold – an increase of 194 from the previous year. In Norway, it is mostly men who purchase international magazines.

Sports

Over 1.7 million Norwegians – or almost 40 % of the population – take active part in sports, either as athletes, trainers or leaders. The Norwegian Sports Federation is enjoying a continually increasing membership, in a time when many other kinds of organisations are experiencing reductions in membership. The Football Federation is the largest special federation with 275,000 members in 1999, followed by skiing and handball. Golf is the fastest growing individual sport.

Sports for the disabled are on the increase, and Norwegian athletes have done very well internationally. During the winter Olympics for the disabled (Paralympics) in Lillehammer in 1994, Norway won the most medals (27 gold – 22 silver – 12 bronze), in front of Germany (22–18–16) and the USA (10–5). Ridder-rennet (blind cross-country competitors with sighted guides) at Beitostølen was the model for "Skiing for Light".

The Birthplace of Skiing

Norway is regarded as the birthplace of the modern sport of skiing. Norwegian athletes are still among the

Bjørn Dæhlie has won the most cross-country ski championships.

best, and Norway has won 236 medals in the Winter Olympics from 1924–1998 (83 Gold, 85 Silver and 68 Bronze medals). Only the former Soviet Union and Unified Germany have had better records. Norway was second best of all nations participating in the Winter Olympics, on home ground in Lillehammer 1994 (10 Gold, 11 Silver and 5 Bronze medals), and also second best in Nagano in 1998 (10-10-5).

Our best known cross-country skier, Bjørn Dæhlie, is the highest winning competitor in the Winter Olympics throughout history. He has also won the most World Championship medals in history (9 gold, 5 silver and 3 bronze).

More than 100,000 spectators attend the Holmenkollen Ski Festival, and on Holmenkollen Sunday about 60,000 enthusiastic fans turn out to watch the ski jumping competition.

Alpine Success

Traditionally, Norway's best competitive athletes are within the Nordic disciplines like cross-country, long jump or a combination thereof. However, in recent years Norwegians have been among some of the best alpine skiers in the world, and the sport is becoming more and more popular. Norway's Lasse Kjus won the alpine over-all World Cup title in 1995/96. In the World Championship in Vail in 1999, he won two gold medals and three silver medals. Kjetil André Aamodt won the World Cup in 1998/99.

Norway also has a long tradition of skating. The most famous Norwegian speed-skater internationally is, with-

Norway has become a noteworthy in international football. Øyvind Leonhardsen is featured here in a duel with the Brazilian player Dunga during the 1998 World Cup Championship in France. Norway beat Brazil 2–1 in a game that Norwegian sports enthusiasts will never forget.

Athletics for the disabled is an important aspect of Norwegian sports. Ragnhild Myklebust was one of the many Norwegian gold medal winners during the 1998 Paralympics in Nagano, and she is the most successful Paralympic competitor of our time, having won 17 gold medals.

out doubt, Johann Olav Koss, who won three gold medals at the Lillehammer Olympics, and set three world records as well. Koss donated a large amount of his prize money to the charity organisation Olympic Aid.

Football, a Favourite Sport

As in many other countries, the most popular sport in Norway is football. Success by the national football team during the last seasons has contributed to an even greater public interest. Norway qualified for the 1994 World Championships in the USA and for the 1998 World Championships in France. The national women's team won the World Championships in Sweden 1995, beating Germany 2–0 in the final.

The high point of the season is the Norwegian Cup Final, played at Ullevaal Stadium in Oslo in October.

The Norway Cup is one of the largest football tournaments in the world. The tournament, played in July/August, is a major event for younger football players, and during the course of seven days, more than 3,000 games are played. 1250 teams, or more than 20,000 players from 32 different countries, participated in 1999.

50,000 Women in Waitz Race

Ice hockey, handball and track and field events are also popular spectator sports in Norway. Several world famous track and field athletes participate in the Bislet Games, arranged annually in Oslo at the beginning of July.

Many running events are sponsored in Oslo. The Oslo Marathon, Holmenkollen Relay Race and Sentrum Race usually gather many participants, from the cream of the crop to Sunday joggers. Internationally famous runners like Grete Waitz and Ingrid Kristiansen have inspired many Norwegian girls to put on their jogging shoes, and each year nearly 50,000 women participate in the all-women Grete Waitz Race.

Biographies

Some Famous Norwegians

Roald Amundsen, Arctic Explorer (1872–1928)

Amundsen, following his parents' wishes, was originally a student of medicine. After his parents passed on, however, he abridged his medical studies in order to become an Arctic explorer. Amundsen was the leader for a Belgian expedition to Antarctica from 1897–99. From 1903–06 he led an expedition, with the Arctic ship "Gjøa", that measured the earth's magnetism and localised the magnetic north pole. During this expedition, they collected a large amount of ethnographic artifacts. In August 1906, this team became the first to sail through the North-West Passage.

Roald Amundsen

Amundsen was then able to collect funds for an expedition to the North Pole. When the American Robert Peary reached the pole in 1909, Amundsen was determined to travel to the south. He did not, however, disclose his plans before his team was aboard Nansen's ship "Fram". In one of history's most daring sled-expeditions, Amundsen and four other members of his team reached the South Pole on the 14th of December 1911 – five weeks before the Englishman Robert F. Scott.

This victory provided Amundsen with the possibility of focusing on his life's dream: to investigate unexplored areas of the Arctic. In 1918, he travelled with the specially constructed ship "Maud" to drift with the ice across the North Pole from the east towards the west. Amundsen's plan failed, and after two winters he decided to utilise an aircraft. The two planes he obtained in 1922 crashed, however, but with economic assistance provided by the American Lincoln Ellsworth, two new planes were purchased in 1925. Again, these planes were wrecked. The airship "Norge", constructed in Italy by the engineer Umberto Nobile, was successful, however, and, on the 11th of May 1926, Amundsen-Ellsworth-Nobile's transpolar expedition from Tromsø crossed the North Pole on the 12th of May, landing in Alaska on the 14th of May.

Amundsen's last years were characterised by bitter conflict over who deserved the honour and recognition for the North Pole expedition. In 1928 when Nobile crashed with the airship "Italia" north of Svalbard, Amundsen immediately volunteered for the rescue mission. He set out from Tromsø with the plane "Latham". On the 18th of June 1928 the plane crashed into the sea near Bjørnøya and all six crew-members died. Nobile was later rescued.

Vilhelm Bjerknes, Physicist (1862–1951)

Bjerknes received a professorship first in Stockholm in 1895, then in Oslo, Leipzig, Bergen and again in Oslo in 1932. Bjerknes established a research group called the Bergen School. Under his leadership during and after the first World War, this research group developed new methods for weather forecasting by systematically studying air masses, fronts and pressure systems. Bjerknes carried out early fundamental research of considerable importance for radio technology.

Bjørnstjerne Bjørnson, Author (1832–1910)

Bjørnson's breakthrough came in 1857 with the historical drama "Mellem Slagene". During that same year, he became the artistic leader at the Norwegian Theatre in Bergen. From 1865–67 Bjørnson led the Christiania Theatre in the country's capital. He wrote mainly novels and stories until 1872, inspired by the setting and spirit of the farming community Bjørnson remembered from his childhood. He also wrote several historical dramas that extended his earlier success. After two years in Italy and

Tyrol, he took up residence on a farm in Aulestad, Gausdal in 1875. From 1882–87 Bjørnson lived in Paris.

His poems from the mid-1870's are representative of social conflict and awareness. Bjørnson was active in political life and social debate. In Norway, the final decades of the 1800's are characterised by strong public opinion and opposition.

Bjørnson is one of the most important figures in Norwegian culture and history, but he has not received the same attention outside Norway. In 1903, he received the Nobel Prize for literature.

Gro Harlem Brundtland, Politician (born 1939)

Brundtland was a Norwegian Labour Party politician and international civil servant. She obtained a Bachelor of Medicine and became assistant chief physician from 1968–74. Brundtland was also the Environmental Minister during the years 1974–79. She was elected into parliament in 1977, and became the Norwegian Prime Minister in 1981, 1986–89 and again from 1990–96. She was Vice President of the Labour Party from 1975–81, and President from 1981–92. From 1983–87 she led the World Commission for the Environment and Development (the Brundtland Commission), established by the UN General Secretary. On the 21st of July 1998, she became Director General of the World Health Organisation.

Ole Bornemann Bull, Violinist and Composer (1810–1880)

Bull began studying the violin as a child, and at nine years of age, he performed at a concert in his native town of Bergen. Thereafter, Bull was self-taught in both the violin and in composition. In 1831, he travelled to Paris, and the following year he held a concert that gave him the reputation of a violin virtuoso. In Paris, Bull also heard another great violinist, Niccoló Paganini. In 1834, Bull travelled to Italy where he was highly successful in Bologna. Then, he performed in various parts of western Europe. In June 1838, he visited Norway and was celebrated as a national hero.

In 1843, Bull toured the USA and gave concerts in the largest American cities. In 1849 he performed with the Norwegian fiddler Myllarguten in Christiania (now called Oslo). Myllarguten was one of Norway's leading folk musicians. Bull initiated the construction of a Norwegian theatre in Bergen, which opened in 1850. In 1852, Bull established the Norwegian colony Oleana, or New Norway, in the state of Pennsylvania in the USA. This project, however, was highly unsuccessful, and Bull lost large sums of money.

From 1870, Bull established residence in the USA, but toured extensively and played, for example, by the pyramids in Egypt in 1876. He also visited Norway each summer and owned a country home on Lysøy Island outside Bergen.

As a violinist, Ole Bull was one of the great virtuosos of an era characterised by virtuosos. He was popular all over Europe and the USA. His work as a composer is less comprehensive and significant, but some of his pieces are still cherished and performed.

Bjørn Erlend Dæhlie, Cross-country Skier (born 1967)

As of August 1998, Dæhlie has won ten individual and four relay Norwegian championships. He has also won five World Cups. He was world champion in the 15 km and in relay in 1991, in the 30 km jaktstart and relay in 1993, and relay in 1995. His performance in the Winter Olympic Games in Nagano garnered him the position as the most-winning winter Olympian. He received a gold medal in the 10 km classic, the 50 km freestyle and in the 4x10 km relay. He also received a silver medal in the 15 km freestyle (jaktstart).

Sverre Fehn, Professor (born 1924)

Fehn received his diploma from The National School of Architecture in 1949 and opened his own practice that same year. From 1971–1994, he was a professor at the Architectural College in Oslo. Fehn designed institutional buildings and schools, Norway's pavilion at the 1958 World's Fair in Brussels and the Nordic pavilion at the 1962 Fair in Venice. The North Cape Church (1965) and the Colosseum cinema (1964) are also examples of Fehn's work. He designed the Hamar Bishops' Farm Museum (1972), the permanent exhibition entitled The Norwegian Middle Ages at the Historic Museum (1979), the Norwegian Glacier Museum in Fjærland at Balestrand (1991) and The Aukrust Centre in Alvdal (1996). Today, Fehn is one of Norway's best-known architects and is also internationally renowned. In 1973, he was awarded the Treprisen, in 1997, the prestigious international Pritzkers Architecture Prize and the Heinrich Tessenow Medal. In 1994, Fehn became commander of the St. Olav's Order.

Kirsten Flagstad, Soprano (1895–1962)

Flagstad grew up in a musical household and made her debut in 1913. From 1918–27 she was associated with several opera companies in Oslo. In 1928 she was engaged by The Stora Theatre in Sweden, and was then launched onto the largest opera stages in Europe and the USA. She performed in Bayreut in Germany and at the Metropolitan in New York, and was guest performer at the San Francisco opera and at Covent Garden in London. When the Norwegian Opera was established in 1958, she became its first director.

Kirsten Flagstad possessed a unique illustrious voice and was considered one of the leading Wagner-singers. She was also called "the voice of the century". The Kirsten Flagstad Museum opened in 1985 at her native home, Strandstuen, in the town of Hamar.

Ragnar Anton Kittil Frisch, Macro-Economist (1895–1973)

Frisch was educated as a jeweller, and was an apprentice with the well-known goldsmith, David Andersen, in Oslo. Frisch simultaneously studied economics at the university, originally because it was the shortest university course! He graduated in 1919 and continued he studies abroad, mostly in France. He completed his doctoral studies in Oslo and received a profes-

sorship in 1928 and became assistant professor in 1928. He taught at the Univeristy of Oslo from 1931–65.

Frisch published a large amount of innovative works within the field of economics and mathematical statistics. In the 1930's he supported an active economic policy and recommended increasing national expenditure. Frisch has been awarded several international prizes, including the prestigious Italian Antonio Feltrinelli Prize in 1961. In 1969 Frisch received the first prize in economics in commemoration of Alfred Nobel, together with the Dutchman Jan Tinbergen, "for the development and application of dynamic models for the analyse of economic processes".

Apart from his economic studies, Frisch was always interested in bee keeping, and carried out genetic and statistical studies associated with this activity.

Jan Garbarek, Jazz Saxophonist and Composer (born 1947)

At fifteen years of age, Garbarek aroused attention and interest in his musical ability after being selected as

Jan Garbarek

the best soloist during the Norwegian Championship for amateur jazz musicians. During the 1960's he studied and played with the American composer George Russell. Garbarek has been a bandleader, often for quartets, and has toured around the world. Today, he is considered as on of the foremost performing saxophone artists. Garbarek has recorded several albums and has composed music for ballet, theatre, film and television. In 1998, he was awarded Knight of the First Class of St. Olav's Order.

Ivar Giaever (Giæver), Norwegian-American Physicist (born 1929)

Giaever received his education as a mechanical engineer at Norway's Technical College in 1952. He emigrated to Canada in 1954 and has resided in the USA since 1956. In 1958 he was employed at the General Electric Research laboratory in New York where he worked especially with phenomena related to super-conductivity. This is an electro-magnetic effect that appears in various substances at lower temperatures. Giaever received the Nobel Prize for physics (together with Leo Esaki and Brian Josephson) for his work with theories about semi and super-conductors.

Edvard Hagerup Grieg, Composer (1843–1907)

Grieg received his first musical instruction from his mother before studying at the Music Conservatory in Leipzig from 1858–62. In 1863 Grieg travelled to Copenhagen where he met the Norwegian composer Rikard Nordraak who was very influential on

Grieg's musical career. In Leipzig, Grieg also became engaged to his cousin, the singer Nina Hagerup.

In the autumn of 1866, Grieg took up residence in Christiania (Oslo) as a music teacher and was influential upon the capital's musical life in his role as, amongst others, a conductor. From the summer of 1877 he lived in Hardanger on the West Coast of Norway and moved to Troldhaugen in 1885 – a house outside Bergen. He toured as a pianist and director and became known and loved in Europe's concert halls. In 1898 he arranged the first Norwegian music festival, which was held in Bergen.

Greig was a composer especially known for his numerous piano concertos, including ten booklets with lyrical pieces, and for his songs composed in honour of the literary works of Norwegian and Danish poets. Moreover, on a larger scale, his music belongs to the most popular Scandinavian music from the 1800's, for example, the accompaniment to Ibsen's play "Peer Gynt", and the piano concerto – one of the most popular in the world.

Norwegian folk music was very important to Grieg, and some of his most important pieces, like "Slåtter" opus 72 (from 1902–03) and "Fire Salmer" from 1906, are inspired by Norwegian folk music. Grieg's exclusive and unique harmony has especially influenced impressionist composers.

Jostein Gaarder, Author (born 1952)

Gaarder received his Bachelor of Arts from the University of Oslo in 1976 after studying Nordic, the History of Philosophy and the Science of

Religion. He has been a school-teacher, and from 1981–1991 taught History of Philosophy at the Folkeuniversitetet in Agder. Since the autumn of 1991, Gaarder has been a full-time writer and lecturer. In collaboration with others, Gaarder has published several textbooks in the field of religion and ethics for sixth-form students. He made his debut as a fictional writer in 1986 with the book "Diagnosen og andre noveller", and later published several books for young readers. The internationally successful "Sophie's World" was released in 1991. By June 1998, this book was published in more than forty different languages. Gaarder has received several Norwegian and international prizes for his books. In 1997 Øystein Wiik's and Gisle Kverndokk's musical version of "Sophie's World" made its world debut in Germany. Gaarder and his wife Siri Dannevig have used proceeds from the sale of "Sophie's World" to establish the international environmental award, The Sofie Prize.

Knut Hamsun, Author (1859–1952)

Hamsun was born in Lom in Gudbrandsdalen, but moved to Hamarøy in Nordland at the age of three. The nature of northern Norway greatly impressed him and is an obvious characteristic of his literary work. In 1887, after a series of travels, including two stays in the USA, he published "Den Gaadefulde" under the name Knut Pedersen. His breakthrough, however, came with the publication of the novel "Sult" in 1890. The series of novels and plays Hamsun published throughout the 1890's established his reputation as Norway's newest great author. The best known works from this period include "Pan" (1894), and "Victoria" (1898). During these years, Hamsun travelled a great deal in Finland, Russia, Caucasus and Turkey.

In 1911, Hamsun purchased a farm in Hamarøy and moved back to Nordland. In 1917 the novel "Markens Grøde" was published, and he was awarded the Nobel Prize for literature in 1920. In 1918, he purchased the farm called Nørholm by Grimstad and moved back to southern Norway. Hamsun ran Nørholm like a model farm, but also continued to write actively. During this era, he published his "vagabond" trilogy: "Landstrykere" (1927), "August" (1930) and "Men Livet lever" (1933).

Hamsun supported occupational forces during the second World War, and was severely fined after the war ended. His last book was published in 1949, the autobiographical "Paa gjen-

Knut Hamsun

grodde Stier", illustrating his poetic talent. Hamsun, along with Henrik Ibsen, is Norway's best-known poet, and his books are translated into several languages.

Odd Hassel, Chemist (1897–1981)

Hassel graduated from the University of Oslo in 1920 with chemistry as his principal subject. He continued his studies in Germany in 1922, and in 1924 completed his doctorate in Berlin. He was an associate professor at the University of Oslo from 1925, and from 1934–1964 was professor of physical chemistry.

Originally, Hassel was mainly interested in inorganic chemistry, but his work from 1930 directed itself towards problems associated with molecular structure. He is world renowned for his work with cyclohexane derivatives, their structure and properties. In addition, he studied and solved several other substantial problems within modern structural chemistry. Hassel was honorary doctor at several foreign universities and a member of many scientific institutions. Hassel, together with the Englishman Derek Barton, won the 1962 Nobel Prize in chemistry for his pioneering research concerning organic molecular structure and conformation.

Sonja Henie, Speed Skater and Figure Skater (1912–1969)

Henie participated in three Olympic Games in 1928, 1932 and 1936 and won three gold medals for figure skating. She was world champion ten times, European champion six times and the Norwegian champion eight

Sonja Henie

times before she began her professional career in 1936. Thereafter, she began an acting career in American skating films, and was the star of several ice-skating shows. With her husband Niels Onstad, Sonja Henie established the Sonja Henie and Niels Onstad Foundation, which financed the construction of the Henie-Onstad Art Centre at Høvikodden in Oslo. This cultural centre opened in 1968, and the couple donated their collection of contemporary art to the museum. Henie's collection of awards and trophies are also on exhibition at Høvikodden.

Thor Heyerdahl, Ethnographer and Zoologist (born 1914)

Today, Heyerdahl is one of Norway's best-known scientists. He is also famous for his many impressive expeditions. The first was made in 1947 with a balsa-raft called "Kon-Tiki". The expedition began in the harbour town Callao, Peru and ended in the Tuamotu Islands. The adventure lasted 101 days and covered over 8000 km. The voyage attempted to prove that it was indeed possible for pre-Columbian Indians in South America to use their rafts to reach Polynesia. In 1969 Heyerdahl began a new expedition, this time to sail from Morocco to Barbados with the reed boat "Ra I". The voyage was not a complete success, so he set sail again the following year with the boat "Ra II". With this attempt, Heyerdahl and his crew reached Barbados. The goal of this voyage was to illustrate that ancient civilisations in Egypt and Africa could have brought cultural impulses to the indigenous population of America. The last of these expeditions was carried out with a new reed boat called "Tigris". Heyerdahl sailed from Iraq via Karachi to Djibouti. Although this voyage was not successful, Heyerdahl still achieved his goal: to highlight trade and cultural relations in the ancient Near East.

In addition, Heyerdahl has carried out significant archaeological excavations in the Maldives, on Easter Island and in Peru. He has also been active in international environmental work and has shown specifically how the ocean is subjected to pollution. Both the "Kon-Tiki" raft and "Ra II" are exhibited at the Kon-Tiki Museum in Bygdøy, Oslo.

Trygve Haavelmo, Macro-Economist (1911–1999)

From 1938–39, Haavelmo taught statistics at the University of Oslo. He received a Bachelor of Science in macro-economics, and a doctorate in 1946. In 1939 he travelled to the USA as a Rockefeller-fellow and remained there during the second World War. During his tenure there, he was employed on the Nortra ship and then as a lecturer by the University of Chicago. From 1948–79 he was a professor of macro-economics and statistics at the University of Oslo. Haavelmo has conducted considerable research in the field of econometrics and mathematical economy for many years. His studies, which have critically analysed various general theories, and his mathematical analyses of key issues have given him a leading position in modern economy. Haavelmo was awarded the Nobel Commemorate Prize for economics in 1989.

Henrik Ibsen, Playwright (1828–1906)

Ibsen was a pharmaceutical apprentice in Grimstad for six years. Under the pseudonym Byrnjolf Bjarme, he made his debut with the tragedy in verse

Henrik Ibsen

"Catalina" in 1850. Later, Ibsen taught at Bergen's Norwegian Theatre from 1851–1859, and then became leader of the Christiania Norwegian Theatre until 1862. During these years he wrote several plays based on Norwegian history, like "Kongs-emnerne" in 1863. In 1864 Ibsen travelled to Italy and remained abroad, mostly in Italy and Germany, for twenty-seven years. In 1866, the drama in verse "Brand" was debuted, followed by "Peer Gynt" in 1867. "Samfundets støtter" (1877) introduced the first of several modern dramas like "A Doll's House" (1879), "Gengangere" (1881), "Vildanden" (1884) and "Hedda Gabler" (1890). The works from the 1890's are characterised by personal confession including "Bygmester Solness" (1892) and "John Gabriel Borkman" (1896). During his lifetime, Ibsen was considered as one of the world's great dramatists and innovators. His plays are still performed all over the world.

Lasse Kjus, Norwegian downhill skier (born 1971)

Kjus was Norwegian slalom champion in 1992 and number one in the downhill combination in the Winter Olympic Games in Lillehammer in 1994. He was also World Cup winner for the 1995-96 season and he obtained a silver medal in the downhill and combination (slalom-downhill) in Nagano. Kjus is member of the Bærum Ski Club.

Sissel Kyrkjebø, Singer (born 1969)

Kyrkjebø's first performance on Norwegian television was in 1984 where her light and beautiful voice endeared the public. In 1986 she released her first album entitled "Sissel" which sold 300,000 copies in Norway alone! Her album "Glade Jul" from 1987 was even more successful and over 500,000 copies were sold. The following year she played the role of Maria von Trapp in the musical "The Sound of Music" in Oslo. In 1993, Kyrkjebø married the Danish entertainer Eddie Skoller and took up residence in Denmark. Her international career, however, was just taking off. Her performance during the opening ceremonies of the winter Olympics in Lillehammer in 1994 was broadcast all over the world. In that same year, Kyrkjebø sang together with Placido Domingo and Charles Aznavour in the television concert "A Christmas in Vienna". This performance was later released as a CD. In 1995 she participated in "A Royal Galla" in London, another internationally broadcast performance. In addition, her beautiful voice was heard on the "Titanic" soundtrack, released in 1997.

Today, Sissel Kyrkjebø is one of Norway's most famous singers and her career is still in the early stages.

Trygve Lie, Labour Party Politician and Civil Servant (1896–1968)

After working as a legal civil servant, Lie was employed as a legal consultant for the Norwegian Federation of Trade Unions. From 1935–1946, he held various cabinet posts, for example, Justice and Foreign Minister. In 1946, Lie was chosen as the United Nation's first General Secretary where he carried out fundamental work as an

Trygve Lie

administrator and broker. Due to resistance from the Soviet Union, Lie resigned his position in 1953. From 1955–1963, he was administrative officer of the Oslo and Akershus districts. During the years 1963–1965, Lie became Industry Minister, and then Trade Minister.

Edvard Munch, Painter and Graphic Artist (1863–1944)

The development of Munch's style is noticeable in his earlier works like "Det syke barn" (1886). The paintings from the 1890's, like "Skrik", "Madonna" and "Døden i sykeværelset", are part of a cycle of paintings that he called "Livsfrisen". The subjects and themes from his paintings are also found in his graphic prints. Munch was a controversial artist, perhaps because his motives could be easily associated with the bohemian circle, a group of artists strongly opposed to contemporary bour-

geoisie. Great opposition was raised when Munch, supported by private funds, decorated the University Hall in Oslo in 1910. Although he began to receive acknowledgement in later years, Munch lived rather isolated on his property, Eikely, in Olso.

Munch bequeathed his collection of his art to the municipality of Oslo, and in 1963 a museum was built in Tøyen, Oslo to house his paintings.

Today, Edvard Munch is the most famous Norwegian painter abroad, and he is also one of the few artists who have played an important role in the development of painting as an art form during the 1900's.

Fridtjof Nansen, Scientist, Arctic Explorer and Diplomat (1861–1930)

In 1888 Nansen completed his doctoral studies and presented a dissertation concerning the central nervous system. In that same year, he crossed Greenland on skis. In order to validate new theories concerning the movement of ice formations from Siberia across the Arctic Ocean to Greenland, Nansen decided to drift with the ice. In 1893 he set sail with a special ship called "Fram". From the Siberian coast, he and his crew travelled northeast, but they did not reach the North Pole. Together with Hjalmar Johansen, Nansen proceeded towards the pole on skis. They reached 86° 4' N, further north than anyone had ever been before.

Nansen then became interested in oceanography and initiated the establishment of an international commission for systematic ocean research. He led the commission's central laboratory from its establishment in 1902 until

Fridtjof Nansen

style primarily based on baroque art, especially Caravaggio's and Rembrandt's light and shadowed pictures. Nerdrum's art often possesses social content like the picture "Mordet på Andreas Baader" (1977–78) and "Flyktninger på havet" (1979–80). During the 1980's his work became more characterised by his use of symbolism, for example "Skyen" from 1985. As a leader for neo-romanticism and figurative art, Nerdrum has met resistance, but is now considered to be one of Norway's most renown pictorial artists internationally.

1908. Nansen published several popular scientific works and carried out expeditions, including a trip through northern Siberia in 1913.

Nansen held an important diplomatic role in connection with the dissolution of Norway's union with Sweden in 1905. His diplomatic undertakings continually became more engaging. Nansen was Norway's first ambassador to London. From 1920 until his death, Nansen was delegate to the League of Nations, where he played a leading role. In 1920 he received an assignment from the League's General to lead repatriation efforts for refugees. Later, he led relief work in the Soviet Union for starving refugees and other work in southeastern Europe, especially in Armenia. Nansen received the Nobel Peace Prize in 1922.

Odd Nerdrum, Painter (born 1944)

Nerdrum has painted mainly portraits and larger figurative compositions in a

Arne Nordheim, Composer (born 1931)

Nordheim studied at the Music Conservatory in Oslo, and later continued his musical education in Copenhagen and Stockholm. Nordheim aroused interest in his abilities as a composer in 1954 during his first performance at the Nordic Youth Music Festival in Stockholm, where he presented his string quartet piece "Essay". Nordheim's international breakthrough came in 1957 with "Aftonland". Nordheim emphasises tonal quality in his music and in the 1960's he became interested in electric music, which he studied during a stay in Warsaw. He was also interested in new forms of media like television and music outside concert halls. With the sculptor Arnold Haukeland, Nordheim created a sound-light sculpture that is now located in Erling Stordahls Institute for the Blind in Skjeberg, Østfold.

In 1968, he was awarded the Norwegian Council's Music Prize for "Eco", a piece composed for a soprano, two choirs and an orchestra. In this work, Nordheim was able to simulate electronic tones using regular instruments. His international position is illustrated by the large amount of commissioned work he has received globally. "Greening" (1973) was commissioned by director Zubin Mehta and the Los Angeles Symphony Orchestra, the ballet "Stormen" (1979) for the Schwezinger Festival in Germany, and the cello concerto "Tenebrae" (1980) for Mstislav Rostropovitsj. His latest works include a violin concerto dedicated to Arve Tellefsen, first performed by him in 1997, and a large commissioned work for Trondheim's 1000-year celebration in 1997, the oratory "Nidaros".

Today, Nordheim is Norway's best-known contemporary composer. He has lived in The National Honorary Residence Grotten since 1981.

Liv Ullman, Actress and Director (born 1938)

Ullman's debut came in 1957. She was employed by the Rogaland Theatre from 1958–59, the Norwegian Theatre from 1960–64 and by the National Theatre until 1971. Ullman has had an international acting career, for example, in several of Ingmar Bergman's films and television series. Ullman debuted as a film director for the film "Sofie" in 1992. The film "Kristin Lavransdatter" (1995) also garnered Ullman international success and recognition.

Sigrid Undset, Author (1882–1949)

Undset's debut came in 1907 with the release of the novel about marriage "Fru Martha Oulie". Afterwards, she wrote several novels and collections that portray the lives and plight of contemporary women. Daughter of the famous archaeologist Ingvald Undset, Sigrid Undset was also fascinated with history. Her interest in this subject is readily apparent in her novel about the Middle Ages "Kristin Lavransdatter", which was released in three volumes between 1920 and 1922, and in the two-volume work "Olav Audunssøn" (1925–27). Apart from illustrating her extensive knowledge of history, these novels prove Undset's ability to create a unique sensitivity within her characters that bring these historical figures alive. Her novels have also garnered her international recognition and fame. In 1928, Undset received the Nobel Prize for literature.

Undset converted to Catholicism in 1924. During the second World War she resided in the USA where she held several lectures relaying the plight

Sigrid Undset

of Norwegians to the American people. Her home in Lillehammer, Bjerkebekk, is now a museum.

Grete Waitz, Distance Runner (born 1953)

Waitz became World Marathon Champion in 1983 and won the silver medal during the 1984 Olympic Games. She also won 33 Norwegian championships and has been world champion for cross-country running five times. Waitz has won the New York Marathon and the London Marathon twice, and has set the world record for the 3000 m twice. Including her four unofficial world record marathons, Waitz has been a role model for many female athletes in Norway and throughout the world. In addition, she initiated the popular Grete Waitz Marathon in Oslo for women.

References

Some useful adresses

Embassies and Consulates

Argentina, Embassy
Drammensveien 39 B
0271 Oslo
22 55 24 48

Australia, Consulate
Jernbanetorget 2
Postboks 686 Sentrum
0106 Oslo
22 47 91 70

Austria, Embassy
Ths Heftyes gate 19
0264 Oslo
22 55 23 48

Austria, Consulate General
Ullern allé 20
0381 Oslo
22 52 33 01

Belgium, Embassy
Drammensveien 103 C
0273 Oslo
22 55 22 15

Brazil, Embassy
Sigurd Syrs gate 4
0273 Oslo
22 55 20 29

Bulgaria, Embassy
Tidemands gate 11
0260 Oslo
22 55 40 40

Canada, Embassy
Wergelandsveien 7
0244 Oslo
22 99 53 00

Chile, Embassy
Meltzers gate 5
0257 Oslo
22 44 89 55

China, People's Republic,
Embassy
Tuengen allé 2 B
0374 Oslo
22 14 89 08

Czech Republic, Embassy
Fritzners gate 14
0264 Oslo
22 43 00 02

Denmark, Embassy
Olav Kyrres gate 7
0244 Oslo
22 54 08 00

Egypt, Embassy
Drammensveien 90 A
0273 Oslo
22 44 77 67

Estonia, Embassy
Oscars gate 26 B
0352 Oslo
22 59 98 02

Finland, Embassy
Ths Heftyes gate 1
0264 Oslo
22 43 04 00

Finland, Consulate General
Per Krohgs vei 1
1065 Oslo
22 32 95 00

France, Embassy and Consulate
Drammensveien 69
0271 Oslo
22 44 18 20

Germany, Embassy
Oscars gate 45
0258 Oslo
22 55 20 10

Great Britain, Embassy
Ths Heftyes gate 8
0244 Oslo
23 13 27 00

Great Britain, British Council
Fridtjof Nansens plass 5
0160 Oslo
22 39 61 90

Greece, Embassy
Nobels gate 45
0244 Oslo
22 44 27 28

Guatemala, Embassy and
Consulate
Oscars gate 59
0258 Oslo
22 55 60 04

Honduras, Consulate General
Gjerdrums vei 12
0486 Oslo
22 02 16 00

Hungary, Embassy
Sophus Lies gate 3
0264 Oslo
22 55 24 18

Iceland, Embassy
Stortingsgaten 30
0244 Oslo
22 83 34 35

India, Embassy
Niels Juels gate 30
0272 Oslo
22 55 22 29

Indonesia, Embassy
Gange-Rolvs gate 5
0273 Oslo
22 44 11 21

Iran, Embassy
Drammensveien 88 E
0271 Oslo
22 55 24 08

Ireland, Consulate
Lilleakerveien 2 C
9283 Oslo
22 12 20 00

Israel, Embassy
Drammensveien 82 C
0271 Oslo
22 44 79 24

Italy, Embassy
Inkognitogaten 7
0258 Oslo
22 55 22 33

Japan, Embassy
Parkveien 33 B
0258 Oslo
22 55 10 11

Jordan, Embassy
Malerhaugveien 19/23
Postboks 6456 Etterstad
0605 Oslo
22 68 38 60

Latvia, Embassy
Bygdøy allé 76
0268 Oslo
22 54 22 80

Latvia, Consulate General
Beddingen 8
0250 Oslo
22 01 42 88

Liberia, Consulate General
Haakon VII's gate 5
0161 Oslo
23 23 90 90

Lithuania, Embassy
Gimle terrasse 6
0244 Oslo
02 55 81 50

Luxembourg, Consulate General
Malerhaugveien 25
Postboks 6155 Etterstad
0602 Oslo
22 08 80 00

Madagascar, Consulate General
Hauges gate 36
3019 Drammen
32 89 30 60

Malaysia, Consulate
Karl Johans gate 27
0159 Oslo
22 40 05 00

Mali, Consulate
Niels Juels gate 11 B
Postboks 1373 Vika
0114 Oslo
22 55 17 79

Mauritius, Consulate
Arbins gate 3
0253 Oslo
22 95 55 00

Monaco, Consulate
Inkognitogaten 33
0258 Oslo
22 12 80 30

Nepal, Consulate General
Haakon VII's gate 5
0161 Oslo
22 83 55 10

Netherlands, Embassy
Oscars gate 29
0244 Oslo
22 60 21 93

New Zealand, Consulate General
Billingstadsletta 19 B
Postboks 113
1376 Billingstad
66 77 53 30

Panama, Consulate General
Akersgaten 18
0158 Oslo
22 42 76 00

Poland, Embassy
Olav Kyrres plass 1
0273 Oslo
22 43 00 15

Portugal, Embassy
Josefines gate 37
0351 Oslo
23 33 28 50

Romania, Embassy
Oscars gate 51
0258 Oslo
22 44 15 12

Russia, Embassy
Drammensveien 74
0271 Oslo
22 55 32 78

Singapore, Consulate General
Veritasveien 1
Postboks 300
1323 Høvik
67 57 97 60

Slovakia, Embassy
Cort Adelers gate 14
0244 Oslo
22 55 55 90

South Africa, Embassy
Drammensveien 88 C
Postboks 2822 Solli
0204 Oslo
23 27 32 20

South Korea, Embassy
Inkognitogaten 3
0258 Oslo
22 55 20 18

Sweden, Embassy
Nobels gate 16 A
0268 Oslo
22 44 38 15

Switzerland, Embassy
Bygdøy allé 78
0268 Oslo
22 43 05 90

Thailand, Embassy
Eilert Sundts gate 4
0259 Oslo
22 12 86 60

Thailand, Consulate General
Dagaliveien 19
Postboks 7 Slemdal
0710 Oslo
22 14 76 65

Tunisia, Consulate General
Solliveien 2 A
Postboks 323
1326 Lysaker
67 53 05 07

Turkey, Embassy
Halvdan Svartes gate 5
0244 Oslo
22 44 99 20

USA, Embassy
Drammensveien 18
0255 Oslo
22 44 85 50

Venezuela, Embassy
Drammensveien 82
Postboks 7638 Skillebekk
0205 Oslo
22 43 06 60

Yugoslavia, Embassy
Drammensveien 105
0273 Oslo
22 44 81 05

Most Visited Museums and Collections

Buskerud
Blaafarveværket
3370 Vikersund
32 78 28 00
www.blaa.no/eng/

Oslo
Skimuseet, Holmenkollen
Kongeveien 5
0787 Oslo
22 92 32 64
www.skiforeningen.no/hk/
tourist/skimus.htm

Oslo
Norsk Folkemuseum
Museumsveien 10
0287 Oslo
22 12 36 66
www.norskfolke.museum.no

Oslo
Kon-Tiki Museet
Bygdøynesveien 36
0286 Oslo
23 08 67 67
www.media.uio.no/kon-
tiki/indeks.shtml

Oslo
Fram-Museet
Bygdøynesveien 36
0286 Oslo
22 43 83 70

Oslo
Vikingskipshuset
Huk Aveny 35
0287 Oslo
22 43 83 79
www.ukm.uio.no/
vikingskipshuset/index.html

Østfold
Fredrikstad Museum
Mindre-Alvs vei 5
69 30 68 75
www.hiof.no/
fredrikstad-museum/

Østfold
Fredriksten Festning
1752 Halden
69 18 67 90
www.hiof.no/fredriksten/

Amusement Parks and Entertainment Centres

Akershus
Norgesparken TusenFryd &
VikingLandet
Mosseveien
1407 Vinterbro
64 97 64 97
www.tusenfryd.no

Buskerud
Sudndalen Lekeland
3577 Hovet
32 08 85 32

Hedmark
Skarnes Lekeland
Slobrua
2100 Skarnes
62 96 10 03

Hordaland
Akvariet i Bergen
Nordnesbakken 4
5005 Bergen
55 55 71 71
www.akvariet.com

Nord-Trøndelag
Namsskogan Familiepark
7892 Trones
74 33 37 00

Oppland
Hunderfossen Familiepark
2625 Fåberg
61 27 72 22
www.hunderfossen.no

Oppland
Lilleputthammer
2636 Øyer
61 27 73 35

Rogaland
Kongeparken
4330 Ålgård
51 61 71 11
www.kongeparken.no

Telemark
Telemark Sommarland
3800 Bø Telemark
35 95 16 99

Telemark
Vierli Vinterland
(akeland)
3864 Rauland
35 07 23 00

Troms
Polar Zoo
Salangsdalen
9250 Bardu
77 18 41 14

Vest-Agder
Kristiansand Dyrepark
4609 Kardemomme by
38 04 97 00
www.dyreparken.com

Other Places of Interest

Finnmark
Nordkapphallen – The North
Cape
9764 Nordkapp
78 47 68 60

Hedmark
Magnor Glassverk – Glass-works
Grenseveien
2240 Magnor
62 83 35 00
www.magnor-glassverk.no/

Hordaland
Fløibanen
Vetrlidsallmenningen 21
5014 Bergen
55 31 48 00

Oppland
Hadeland Glassverk – Glass-works
Glassverksveien 9
Postboks 85
3521 Jevnaker
61 31 64 00
www.hadeland-glassverk.no

Sogn og Fjordane
Flåmsbana – The Flåm Railway
Aurland
57 63 21 00 (booking information)
www.flaamsbana.no/

Sør-Trøndelag
Nidaros Domkirke – Cathedral
Bispegata 5
7012 Trondheim
73 89 08 00

Contributors to the 25th edition:
Else Brudevold, Kjell Dragnes, Roar Hanssen, Per Egil Hegge, Arve Henriksen, Lars Kluge, Mona Langset, Kjell Paulssen, Jahn Rønne, Henrik Width, Roar Østgårdsgjelten.
Maps, diagrams and drawings: Hans Petter Carlsen, John-Arvid Fosseie.

FACTS ABOUT NORWAY
25th edition
© Chr. Schibsteds Forlag AS, Oslo 2000

Editors: Dag Viggo Nilsen, Kjersti H. Johnsen
Translation: International Language School
Cover: Blå basill as – Bendte Moen
All photographs: SCANPIX, except pp. 58 and 60: Forsvarets rekrutterings- og mediesenter (Military's recruitment and public relations centre)
Typesetting and repro: AIT Otta
Printed and bound by AIT Otta
ISBN 82-516-1773-1